THE GREAT BOOK OF BASKETBALL

Interesting Facts and Sports Stories

Sports Trivia Vol.4

Bill O'Neill

ISBN-13: 978-1981964451

DON'T FORGET YOUR FREE BOOKS

CONTENTS

INTRODUCTION

If you're a fan of basketball, you're in the right place. This book is chock-full of stats, tidbits and sometimes irreverent facts about your favorite NBA teams and players. This book could settle some arguments among your friends about who's the better player. This book could win you a drink at a bar when you pull out the random nugget of information to settle that bet.

This book will have some of the lesser-known back stories about those players and teams that everyone knows about. You'll learn about players who got along, and teammates who didn't. The quips and quotes of famous hoopsters, and hopefully, maybe some new perspectives of players from different eras throughout the history of the NBA.

CHAPTER 1
BACK IN THE DAY

While it's easy to make fun of all that grainy black-and-white footage, what looks like sped-up film and unorthodox shooting styles, there were plenty of reasons the NBA of yesteryear was just as interesting as today's global brand as we know it. There were innovations, star players, dynastic teams, and a little bit of controversy along the way.

The Birth of a League

The NBA as everyone knows it today is far different than its first day of existence on Aug. 3, 1949. The National Basketball Association was actually the merger of two rival leagues, the Basketball Associated of America (BAA) and the National Basketball League (NBL).

The NBL was created in the mid-1930s, but known as the Midwest Basketball Conference. In 1937, it was changed to the National Basketball League. Corporate sponsorship took on a much bigger role in those days as Goodyear, Firestone and General Electric – the original owner of NBC – created the league.

What was originally an informal 10-game season among teams in Midwest cities grew quickly in popularity. The home team could choose the format of either playing in four 10-minute quarters or three 15-minute periods.

The NBL was unopposed until 1946, when the BAA originated. The big selling points for the BAA were they played in large cities, played 48 minutes instead of 40, allowed players a sixth foul and acquired players directly from college.

Both leagues were at risk financially trying to run the other out of business, but in 1949, representatives from both leagues met in New York City at the Empire State Building. There, they agreed to merge together to form the National Basketball Association as a 17-team league under BAA president Maurice Podoloff.

Maurice Podoloff

Podoloff himself is a unique character in sports history because he is the only man to run two professional sports simultaneously. He was also the president of the American Hockey League. Podoloff, though, is more widely known in basketball circles since the NBA's Most Valuable Player is awarded the Maurice Podoloff Trophy at season's end.

Podoloff served as NBA commissioner until 1963, and the native of Ukraine was inducted into the Basketball Hall of Fame in 1974. The man in charge of some of the world's tallest athletes was himself only 5-foot-2.

Danny Biasone and Leo Ferris

If Podoloff is to be given credit for running the NBA, Biasone and Ferris are the ones who arguably saved the league from extinction in the mid-1950s. Biasone was the owner of the Syracuse Nationals (today's Philadelphia 76ers), one of the original teams of the NBL and one of the seven teams that were absorbed into the NBA at the time of the merger.

The league struggled to make headway in the late 1940s, and by the early 1950s, it had contracted to eight teams. The slow pace of play and foul-filled contests after one team raced out to a huge lead turned off many fans, leaving the league in limbo. In the 1950-51 season, the Fort Wayne Pistons defeated the Minneapolis Lakes 19-18, and the teams combined for just four fourth-quarter points.

Biasone and Nationals general manager Leo Ferris tried out their idea for a shot clock during a scrimmage in 1954. Biasone felt an entertaining game in his view was when the teams combined to attempt approximately 120 shots. Ferris took the number of seconds (2,880) in a game, divided by 120, and that's how the 24-second shot clock was born.

George Mikan

George Mikan was one of the primary reasons Biasone devised the shot clock to speed up the game. Mikan, who averaged at least 20.6 points in each of his four NBA seasons as well as 13.5

rebounds per game the first four years the league tracked rebounds as a statistic, was a 6-foot-10, 245-pound giant who dominated in the paint on both ends of the court.

He used his long reach to shoot over smaller players and to block shots defensively, essentially serving as a one-man wall around the basket. In fact, Mikan was so good at blocking shots that the NBA had to create what is now known as the "goaltending rule" in which a player cannot block a shot while the ball is on its way down.

Offensively, Mikan had the rarest of skills, the ability score from close range using either hand. Anyone who has ever tried out for a high school basketball team at some point in their lives has done the "Mikan Drill," in which a player shoot layups, alternating with each hand, and using the basket as a shield while not letting the rebound touch the floor.

Mikan's Lakers won four of the first five NBA titles in league history and also set a precedent for the league's penchant of having dynasties that continues to this day.

Red Auerbach

Forever associated with the Boston Celtics and his trademark victory cigars after winning a grand total of 16 titles as coach, general manager or president of the team, Auerbach got his start further south on the East Coast with the Washington Capitols in the BAA. He made the playoffs all three years there, but failed to win a title.

Auerbach also had a one-season stint with the Tri-Cities Blackhawks in the NBA's inaugural 1949-50 season. He went 28-29 and resigned after owner Ben Kerner traded away John Mahnken, whom Auerbach considered his best player.

Auerbach was hired by the Celtics mainly because then-owner Walter Brown asked for recommendations from the local media, and they suggested him. Auerbach is also credited with breaking down the NBA's racial barrier by selecting Chuck Cooper in the second round of the 1950 draft. Cooper was the first African-American to be selected by an NBA team, and by 2015, almost three of every four players in the NBA (74.4 percent) were African-American – the highest of any major professional sports leagues in the U.S. and Canada. Auerbach is also credited with being the first coach to have a starting five of all African-Americans, beginning a game with Bill Russell, Willie Nauls, Tom Sanders, Sam Jones and K.C. Jones in 1964. He also made Russell the first African-American coach in North American pro sports when he tabbed the center as a player-coach for the 1967-68 season.

Bob Cousy

Auerbach was the architect of the second dynasty of the NBA, but one that lasted far longer with nine titles in a 10-year span. While almost everyone can tick off the names of the Celtics stars

– Cousy, Sharman, Russell, Sanders, Havlicek, Heinsohn, Ramsay and Jones – Auerbach wasn't sold on Cousy at first.

Many expected Cousy to be Auerbach's first pick in the 1950 draft, but he wanted no part of the point guard who led Boston-area school Holy Cross to the 1947 NCAA Tournament title. Auerbach opted for center Charlie Share with the No. 1 overall pick and famously asked the local media, "Am I supposed to win, or please the local yokels?" in defending his selection.

Cousy went third to the Tri-Cities Blackhawks, but he did not report because he was trying to get a driving school off the ground in Worcester, Massachusetts, and had no desire to relocate to that part of the Midwest. The Chicago Stags – the city's precursor to the Chicago Bulls – acquired his draft rights in a trade, but the team folded before the 1950-51 season after just four years in existence

Cousy was awarded to Boston in a dispersal draft, but the flashy style Auerbach originally had no use for became viable because Cousy could quickly move the ball in a loaded Celtics offense that included Hall of Famers Ed Macauley and Bill Sharman. The trio would revolutionize the NBA further through fast-break basketball and create the foundation for what is the best dynasty in league history.

Bill Russell

The Celtics' dynasty didn't really begin until Auerbach acquired

Russell after the St. Louis Hawks selected him No. 2 in the 1956 draft. The deal almost never came to fruition, though, because after originally agreeing to send Ed Macauley to St. Louis for the rights to Russell, Hawks owner Ben Kerner wanted more.

Kerner and Auerbach had a contentious history – Auerbach resigned after one season in Tri-Cities following a trade Kerner made without Auerbach's knowledge, and the Celtics also had Kerner's former top pick Bob Cousy after the guard refused to sign with the team when it was located in Tri-Cities. To complete the Russell trade, Kerner wanted Cliff Hagan, picked by the Celtics in 1953 who had yet to play because he was drafted into the military.

Auerbach signed off the deal and acquired Russell, and later selected his San Francisco teammate K.C. Jones and Tommy Heinsohn that year. Though Russell did not join the team until midseason because he was also part of the 1956 U.S. Olympic team, he more than made up for that lost time as he averaged 14.7 points and a league-high 19.6 rebounds in leading the Celtics to their first NBA title.

It was the beginning of an incredible career that resulted in 11 NBA titles over 13 seasons as a player and coach that also included five MVP awards – only Michael Jordan has more. Additionally, in 2009, the NBA announced it was going to name the NBA Finals MVP Award after Russell.

Tom Heinsohn

These days, Heinsohn is still the beloved Celtics television announcer who gives out "Tommy Points" for hustle and clutch plays, but Heinsohn holds a unique spot in the team's history. He is the only person that was with the Celtics in some official capacity – player, coach or otherwise – for all 17 of their NBA titles and all 21 NBA Finals appearances.

While Heinsohn and Bill Russell were good teammates, they were not – and still are not – particularly close. Russell felt he deserved the 1957 NBA Rookie of the Year award more than Heinsohn and told him publicly he deserved half of the $300 bonus that came with the award. Heinsohn also made an autograph request of Russell for a family member the center never fulfilled. The two simply had a pure basketball working relationship and little else.

By the time Heinsohn's playing career ended in 1965, Auerbach wanted him to take the Celtics coaching reins. But Heinsohn refused because he felt he wouldn't be able to control Russell given the lack of a relationship between the two. It was Heinsohn who suggested to Auerbach he make Russell player-coach given how the center had the basketball acumen to do both roles.

Heinsohn eventually took the Celtics' coaching job three seasons later, after Russell retired, and led Boston to the 1973-74 title.

Bob Pettit

Despite their dynasty, the Celtics did not own a monopoly on the NBA's greatest players. Bob Pettit was one of those stars, with a basketball start that harkens another of the game's greats – Micahel Jordan.

Pettit grew up in Louisiana, where he was cut from his high school's varsity teams both his freshman and sophomore years. But a five-inch growth spurt, coupled with a work ethic his father helped instill, Pettit led his high school to a state title as a junior.

After a standout career at LSU in which he was a two-time All-American, he was the second overall pick in the 1954 draft by the Milwaukee Hawks, yet another stop in the nomadic franchise's history. Pettit's $11,000 salary was the highest by an NBA draft pick at the time.

Berner realized Pettit was too small to be a center in the NBA and moved him to forward. His speed at the position, which he used to be one of the best offensive rebounders in league history, resulted in a standout 11-year career in which he averaged 26.4 points and 16.2 rebounds and the 1958 NBA title over the Celtics.

Pettit scored a playoff-record 50 points in that series-clinching victory, which is the only reason why the Celtics did not reel off 10 straight titles from 1957-66 and why the Hawks reached the

NBA finals four times in a five-year span from 1957-61.

Wilt Chamberlain

One can't talk about Bill Russell without Wilt Chamberlain, they are the yin and the yang of the early NBA and pioneers along with George Mikan at the center position. And Chamberlain was everything Russell was not when you consider the statistical superlatives he achieved while being denied an NBA title until later in his career.

The Philadelphia Warriors were actually Chamberlain's second professional team. His first was the Harlem Globetrotters, with whom he played from 1958-59. The NBA did not accept players into the draft before the completion of the graduating class, and Chamberlain had no interest in returning to Kansas following an inconsistent junior season. So he signed a $50,000 contract with the Globetrotters, with the highlight of his year barnstorming a meeting with then-Russian prime minister Nikita Khrushchev.

Chamberlain broke eight NBA records his rookie season and was the first player in league history to be named NBA MVP and Rookie of the Year in the same season. Only Wes Unseld equaled that feat in 1969. It took Chamberlain all of 56 games to set the single-season points record and he finished his rookie season averaging 37.6 points and 27.0 rebounds.

Chamberlain's career shooting percentage (54.0 percent) was better than his free throw percent (51.1). In the 1966-67 season, when he won his first NBA title, the difference was a career-high 24.2 percent as he shot 68.3 percent from the floor and 44.1 percent from the line.

RANDOM FACTS AND FIGURES

1. During their dynasty of 11 titles in 13 years, the Celtics averaged 55.07 wins as the length of the NBA season went from 72 games to 75 (1959-60) to 79 (1960-61) to 80 (1961-62) to 81 (1966-67) to the current 82-game format (1967-68). Only once, during their last title-winning season in 1968-69, did the Celtics have a winning percentage of less than .600.

2. It took the Hawks' franchise nine years to have as many playoff series wins as city locations (3 – Tri-Cities, Milwaukee, Atlanta).

3. How important was the introduction of the 24-second shot clock? Teams combined to average 79 points in the 1953-54 season, the last one before it was introduced. In 1954-55, that number jumped to 93 points. By 1957, the figured jumped another 14 points to 107.

4. Despite his offensive prowess via his ambidextrous ways around the basket, George Mikan was a career 40.4 percent shooter from the field. He did, however, shoot 78.2 percent from the foul line.

5. How much did Red Auerbach and Ben Kerner dislike each other? In the 1957 NBA Finals, Auerbach was fined $300 for

punching Kerner in Game 3.

6. Bill Russell's defense was so good the Celtics jokingly referred to it as the "Hey, Bill!" defense because it would often take place when a defender got beat and would yell to Russell to rotate over to help and use his height to affect the shot.

7. Bob Cousy never shot 40 percent from the field in a season despite averaging almost 18 attempts per game. But he did lead the NBA in assists for eight straight seasons from 1952-60.

8. One of the reasons Bill Russell lasted until the No. 2 pick was because of the Ice Capades. Celtics owner Walter Brown was also president of the Ice Capades and he promised Rochester Royals owner Lee Harrison, whose team held to the No. 1 pick, that he would send the Ice Capades to Rochester for a show if they didn't select Russell.

9. Dolph Schayes, who won the 1955 NBA title with the Syracuse Nationals, averaged a double-double in points and rebounds every season throughout the 1950s.

10. There were 17 teams when the NBA played its first season in 1949-50. The second season started with just 11 after three teams left for the ill-fated National Professional Basketball League and three teams folded. A seventh team, the Washington Capitols, folded 35 games into the season.

11. The Eastern Division in the 1952-53 season was incredibly top-heavy. New York, Syracuse and Boston were separated by 1 ½ games as they combined for 140 wins. The other two teams – Baltimore and Philadelphia – were a cumulative 28-111 while going 2-47 on the road.

12. Maurice Stokes could have been one of the best players in NBA history had he not suffered a seizure on the team's flight from Detroit to Cincinnati following a playoff game in 1958. In his three seasons, Stokes averaged 16.4 points and 17.3 rebounds.

13. Wilt Chamberlain actually took a pay cut with his first NBA deal. After making $50,000 for his one season with the Harlem Globetrotters, he made $30,000 in his first season with the Philadelphia Warriors, who made him the highest-paid player in the league with that deal.

14. Like George Mikan before him, Chamberlain was so dominant offensively he forced NBA rules changes. While the more well-known one was the widening of the lane, the league also banned him from making free throws by dunking. Yes, Chamberlain was so long and so athletic he was able to dunk from the foul line without a running start.

15. At their absolute best, the Celtics averaged a club-record 124.5 points in the 1959-60 season. Five players – Tom Heinsohn, Bob Cousy, Bill Sharman, Bill Russell and Frank Ramsay – all scored more than 1,000 points that season.

It's the fourth-highest average in NBA history, eclipsed only by two of Wilt Chamberlain's teams (1961-62 and 1966-67) and the 1981-82 Denver Nuggets, who averaged 126.5 points... and gave up 126.0 per game.

TRIVIA TIME

1. How many times did the Celtics beat the Hawks to win the NBA Finals during their 13-year dynasty?

    A. 1
    B. 2
    C. 3
    D. 4

2. How many times was Tommy Heinsohn elected to the NBA All-Star Game?

    A. 3
    B. 6
    C. 5
    D. 9

3. From 1959-1960 to 1967-78, Bill Russell and Wilt Chamberlain won all but one NBA MVP award. Who won the one they didn't?

    A. Oscar Robertson
    B. Tom Heinsohn
    C. Bob Cousy
    D. Bob Pettit

4. What was George Mikan's highest single-season scoring average?

   A. 31.4
   B. 27.6
   C. 28.0
   D. 28.4

5. Which of these players DID NOT average 30 points per game in at least two seasons prior to 1970?

   A. Elgin Baylor
   B. Oscar Robertson
   C. Jerry West
   D. Rick Barry

ANSWERS:

1. C
2. B
3. A
4. D
5. D.

CHAPTER 2

THE AMERICAN BASKETBALL
ASSOCIATION (ABA)

Even with an established dynasty in the Boston Celtics and a parade of stars in Cousy, Heinsohn, Russell and Chamberlain, there were still plenty of people ready to challenge the National Basketball Association as the top league for hoops in the country. After all, unlike its football, baseball and hockey counterparts, the NBA was still a relatively young league – it was heading towards early adulthood as the 1970s approached.

Having fended off the fledgling American Basketball League in the early 1960s; the league had only one full season in 1961-62 and folded during the 1962-63 season, the NBA had the game to itself for five seasons before the next rival league would take form. That would be the American Basketball Association, whose legacy continues today in the NBA.

A Grand Plan

The owners of the 11 teams that comprised the ABA didn't have breaking up the NBA as a goal. To the contrary, their end game was to join the more established league. That was a selling point to potential owners as the league was formed, that it would be cheaper to form a rival league than pay the league an expansion fee as a new NBA franchise.

What the ABA lacked in terms of established publicity, it aggressively sought with its distinctive on-court aesthetics. Start with the ball, which was red, white and blue as opposed to the NBA's orange. It opted for a 30-second shot clock in comparison to the NBA's 24-second one. But the ABA's lasting legacy is making the 3-point line part of basketball at every level, though it was something the ABL utilized in its brief existence.

Chaos at the Top

While the ABA's first commissioner was former NBA great George Mikan, who introduced both the 3-point line and multi-colored basketball, he wound up being one of seven commissioners in the league's nine years of existence.

Mikan served as commissioner from 1967-69 before resigning and giving way to James Carson Gardner. His biggest claim to fame was moving the Houston Mavericks to North Carolina in 1969, with the Cougars playing in Charlotte shortly after he failed to secure a second term in the U.S. House of Representatives. In the end, it was another former NBA great, Dave DeBusschere, who took over as commissioner in 1975 and helped negotiate the deal that led to the ABA-NBA merger the following year.

Traveling Shoes

Nearly all 11 teams that took the court in 1967 for the ABA's inaugural season wound up making at least one move to a different city, state or region. In fact, only two teams _ the Indiana Pacers and Kentucky Colonels _ stayed in one place in league history. And of the 11, four were part of the 1976 merger with the NBA.

The Pacers were arguably the most successful ABA franchise, winning three titles and reaching the finals on two other occasions. They had three different MVPs in their title-winning campaigns, first swingman Roger Brown in 1970, then guard Freddie Lewis in 1972 and forward-center George McGinnis the following year.

The New York Nets were the only other team to win multiple ABA titles, doing so first in 1974 and again in the league's final season in 1976. The Kentucky Colonels reached the finals three times in a five-year span from 1971-75, finally breaking through for their only title in 1975 by denying the Pacers a fourth ABA crown.

The Colonels, who played at Freedom Hall in Louisville, also had the best single season in ABA history, going 68-16 in 1971-72 and winning the Eastern Division by a whopping 23 games over the Virginia Squires. Center Artis Gilmore, standing an imposing 7-foot-3, won Rookie of the Year and MVP honors by averaging 23.8 points, 17.8 rebounds and 5.0 blocks. He and Dan Issel formed a lethal tandem as Issel, a former collegiate standout down the road in Lexington at Kentucky, averaged 30.6 points and 11.2 rebounds.

But that team was bounced in six games in the divisional semifinals by the New York Nets. Kentucky lost the first two games at home by double-digit margins and never recovered, bowing out in six.

Franchise movement, save Indiana and Kentucky, was a defining hallmark of the ABA. While the Dallas Chaparrals stayed in-state and eventually became the San Antonio Spurs, the Houston Mavericks became the Carolina Cougars and then moved to St. Louis in 1974.

The Denver Nuggets franchise originally started in Kansas City, but never played a game there. They were also known as the Denver Larks, and then the Rockets before switching to the Nuggets in 1974. The ABA had a franchise in Florida, the Miami Floridians, that had its roots in Minnesota.

Will Ferrell's comedy movie "Semi-Pro" includes a fictional ABA team called the Flint Tropics that he was trying to include in the NBA merger, working out an agreement with the league's commissioner that the top four teams would be the ones that would go to the NBA. Former ABA stars Gilmore and George Gervin have cameo roles.

The ABA had two franchises in Minnesota in its brief history as the Muskies were there for the league's first season before bolting to Miami, and then the Pittsburgh Pipers set up a shot for one season before returning to western Pennsylvania for the 1969-70 season.

The Shrewd Spirit of St. Louis

By the time the Spirits arrived in St. Louis in 1974, it was the team's third city after previous stops in Houston (Mavericks) and Carolina (Cougars). The club was also on their second set of owners as James Gardner had bought the team from a group led by T.C. Morrow and had then-Houston Oilers owner Bud Adams as a minority partner.

The team spent two seasons in St. Louis, and was originally headed to a fourth city _ Salt Lake City _ to play in Utah before folding with the ABA-NBA merger. The Spirits and Kentucky Colonels each negotiated different buyouts with the NBA; Colonels owner John Y. Brown used his money to stay in basketball and bought the Buffalo Braves.

The Spirit ownership went a different route, folding the franchise and worked out an agreement in which they would receive a percentage of TV revenue from the four ABA teams joining the NBA in perpetuity. Over the next 38 years, this deal pocketed a cool $300 million for the ownership group. But that paled in comparison to the final payoff in which the ownership group agreed to a one-time, $500 million payout in 2014 in exchange for ending future payments.

Julius Erving

While the lack of a television contract ultimately led to the downfall of the ABA, it sure wasn't due to the lack of star power on the court. There were many players who were crossover stars in both leagues, including Issel, George Gervin, Connie Hawkins, Rick Barry and Gilmore, but none were more famous than a small forward from the University of Massachusetts. While he was named Julius Erving, he is better known as "Dr. J."

Erving led the ABA in scoring three times, once with the Virginia Squires and twice with the New York Nets. He is directly entwined with the fates of those two franchises, because once the Squires traded him following the 1972-73 season, they were never the same and eventually folded at the time of the merger.

The Nets, meanwhile, became one of the league's best teams and one of the four who would be taken into the NBA.

Erving spent only two seasons at the University of Massachusetts, where he averaged 26.3 points and 20.2 rebounds. He remains one of only six players to average at least 20 points and 20 rebounds in NCAA history.

Because he left after two seasons, the ABA was Erving's only option since NBA draft rules made no contingencies for players leaving college early. He signed with the Virginia Squires as a free agent and averaged 27.3 points as a rookie and helped them to the East Division finals.

Now eligible to enter the NBA draft, Erving somehow lasted until the 12th pick overall and was taken by the Milwaukee Bucks. One could only wonder what could have been had Erving signed with the Bucks and joined Oscar Robertson and Kareem Abdul-Jabbar. Erving instead signed with the Hawks before the draft because his former agent deceived him into signing a low-value contract.

There were three teams in two leagues vying for his services, and eventually, the U.S. court system had to intervene. Erving played three exhibition games with the Hawks before a three-judge panel ruled he belonged to the Squires. The NBA also fined the Hawks for signing him since the Bucks owned Erving's draft rights.

None of these distractions bothered Erving on the court as he averaged 31.9 points for the Squires. But the poor finances of the franchise forced them to trade Erving to the Nets before the 1973-74 season. With Erving leading the charge, the Nets won their first ABA title in 1974 and then the last ABA title two years later against the Nuggets. Erving averaged 34.7 points in that postseason and was in the top 10 of almost every category in the regular season.

George Gervin

The man was so cool he was known as "The Iceman." George Gervin didn't need those flashy dunks Erving made popular, he would simply glide to the basket and often finish with a finger roll or a layup. But before arriving in the ABA, Gervin had made an interesting name for himself in college.

He originally began at Long Beach State, where a young coach named Jerry Tarkanian was building a successful program. But Gervin, a Detroit native, was homesick and returned to Michigan before the end of the first semester. He would then enroll at Eastern Michigan and averaged 29.5 points in the 1971-72 season.

But he was far from being "The Iceman" at this point. In fact, he was the complete opposite. Gervin punched a player from Roanoke College in Eastern Michigan's College Division semifinals, earning himself a suspension and eventual removal from the team. His invites to the 1972 Olympic and Pan-Am Games teams were also rescinded, which leads one to wonder whether or not the U.S. team would have been in a position to be upset by the Soviet Union in the gold medal game had Gervin made the national squad.

Gervin came to the Squires by way of the Pontiac Chaparrals of the Eastern Basketball Association. It was another case of a star-crossed cameo as Squires scout and eventual Bulls and Suns head coach Johnny "Red" Kerr was responsible for bringing Gervin to the mid-Atlantic.

For one season, Gervin and Erving played together in the ABA, and the two would duel after practice. Gervin credited those games into making him a better player as his career arc began with one of the best players in the ABA in Erving and ended with one of the best in the NBA as he was teammates with a young Michael Jordan with the Bulls.

Dan Issel

After a standout career at Kentucky in which he set (and still holds) the school record with 2,138 points, Issel had a choice to make for his professional career. He was drafted in the eighth round by the Detroit Pistons in the 1970 NBA draft, or he could continue playing in the comforts of Kentucky after the Colonels made him the fourth overall pick.

Issel dominated the league throughout his six seasons, leading the league in scoring on three occasions. He teamed with 7-foot-2 center Artis Gilmore to form a devastating tandem as the Colonels won the 1975 ABA title. His reward for winning the title was being dealt to the Baltimore Claws, but since that team folded before the start of the 1975-76 season, he was then traded to Denver.

That started a highly successful 10-year run in which the Nuggets joined the NBA as part of the merger and became a perennial playoff contender in the 1980s under former ABA player Doug Moe. A seven-time All-Star, Issel finished his professional career with 27,482 points, which ranks 11th overall when combining points from both leagues. His 12,823 points in the ABA trail only fellow Kentucky alum and one-time teammate

Louie Dampier.

Spencer Haywood

He may have been a one-year wonder in the ABA, but that was more than enough time for Haywood to make his case as one of the league's best players. Haywood set the precedent Erving followed by leaving college after two years – Haywood was the first "hardship case" who left school early after averaging 32.1 points and 21.5 rebounds for Detroit in the 1968-69 season – and signed with the Rockets, turning them into instant contenders.

Haywood averaged 30.0 points and 19.5 rebounds en route to being the league's Rookie of the Year and MVP in 1970. He was also the All-Star Game MVP after totaling 23 points, 19 rebounds and seven blocks for the West. Haywood would win an NBA title in 1980 with the Los Angeles Lakers, but he was also suspended for the final four games of the NBA Finals by coach Paul Westhead due to his struggles with a cocaine addiction.

The Squires' Sell-Off

Despite carrying the label of the Virginia Squires, the team never really had a home as it was one of the ABA's "regional" franchises. Home games were in one of four locations – Richmond, Hampton, Norfolk and Roanoke. And the Virginia area was the third stop for a franchise that originated in Oakland

and moved to the nation's capital for the 1969-70 season.

Earl Foreman bought the team from singer Pat Boone and moved it to Washington. While the Squires was always considered one of the teams that were part of the ABA-NBA merger when talks began in 1970, Bullets owner Abe Pollin was able to get the ABA owners to convince Foreman to move to Virginia to help the merger cause.

Foreman, though, constantly struggled with the team's finances and often had to jettison with star players. In 1970, he traded Rick Barry to the New York Nets for a draft pick and $200,000 to help balance the books. Despite dealing away the disgruntled superstar, the Squires won the East by 11 games.

The following year they drafted Erving and reached the second round of the semifinals. While Gervin and Erving were on the same team in the 1972-73 season, coach Al Bianchi rarely played them together until late in the season, and the Squires made a first-round exit at the hands of Kentucky.

Foreman sold Erving to the Nets prior to the 1973-74 season and then unloaded Gervin to the Spurs during the 1974 All-Star break. ABA commissioner Mike Storen tried to block the deal claiming it was not in the best interest of the league, but the deal went through as Gervin was sold for $225,000.

Those two deals doomed the franchise, which went a combined 30-137 the next two seasons. At one point, a player sued the team after a paycheck bounced. The Squires survived the 1975-76 season only because a local bank loaned Foreman $250,000. By May of 1976, the franchise was canceled by the league after it missed an assessment payment of $75,000. That meant the ownership group would receive no money from the impending merger.

A Coaches' Cradle

The difference in the rules, most notably the 3-point line, had a lasting effect on the game because some of the ABA's best guards would eventually become some of the NBA's best coaches. They included Larry Brown, whose own vagabond ways mirror the league he grew up with. Brown remains the only person to win an NCAA Tournament title and NBA title as a coach, and was elected to the Hall of Fame in 2002.

Hubie Brown led Kentucky to its only ABA title in 1975 and got his first NBA head coaching job with Atlanta two seasons later. A two-time NBA coach of the year, Hubie Brown is also a Hall of Famer with more than 500 wins to his credit.

Billy Cunningham was originally the fifth overall selection by the Philadelphia 76ers in the 1965 NBA draft, but he spent two seasons with the Carolina Cougars and was a fan favorite from his college playing days at North Carolina. Cunningham would then later coach the 76ers, and Erving, to the 1983 NBA title before his eventual induction into the Hall of Fame in 2006.

Doug Moe was an ABA journeyman player who averaged 16.3 points and 6.8 rebounds with four teams over five seasons in the league. After two assistant stints with Carolina and Denver in the ABA, he became the first NBA coach for San Antonio after the merger and got to the Western Conference finals in 1979.

Moe's up-tempo offense didn't have many set plays, it was predicated on quick passing and screens. He returned to Denver in 1980 and coached the Nuggets for 10 seasons, leading the league in scoring six times.

RANDOM FACTS AND FIGURES

1. Only once in the ABA's nine years did its leading scorer average more points than the NBA's top scorer. In the 1968-69 season, Larry Jones averaged 28.4 points for the Denver Nuggets, edging out Elvin Hays' 28.38 mark for the San Diego Rockets.

2. Louie Dampier was one of the few players who not only spanned the ABA's entire nine-year existence but also one of just two players to play for only one team. The seven-time All-Star finished atop the league's scoring annals with 13,726 points despite never leading the ABA in scoring.

3. While many remember Rick Barry for his underhanded shooting style for free throws, he is the only player to lead the ABA, NBA and NCAA in scoring in a single season. He is also one of only four father-son duos to win NBA titles after his son Brent won the 2005 title with the San Antonio Spurs.

4. Erving finished fifth on the ABA's all-time scoring list with 11,662 points despite playing just five seasons in the league.

5. Issel is the only ABA player with two of the league's single-season top-five scoring totals. His league record of 2,538

points in the 1971-72 season would rank tied for 26th when combining the leagues.

6. Only 37 players made 100 or more 3-pointers in ABA history. By comparison, the shot is now so entrenched in the NBA that 91 players hit 100 or more 3-pointers in the 2016-17 season alone.

7. The real reason it took nearly six years to complete the ABA-NBA merger was due to a lawsuit filed in 1970 by the NBA Players Association on behalf of Oscar Robertson that opposed the merger on antitrust grounds. The upshot of the lawsuit was that player salaries increased in both leagues before it was settled in 1976.

8. In the last three seasons before the mergers, teams from each league squared off in the preseason. The ABA won 62 of the 96 games, highlighted by the 1975 ABA champion Kentucky Colonels topping the NBA champion Golden State Warriors.

9. The ABA was forced to scrap its divisional format in the 1975-76 season because both the San Diego Sails and Utah Stars were forced to fold during the season due to financial difficulties.

10. The Chicago Bulls were one of the biggest opponents to the Colonels, being one of the four teams in the merger because they held the NBA draft rights to center Artis Gilmore. Colonels owner John Y. Brown folded the team for

$3 million and eventually sold Gilmore's rights to the Bulls for another $1.1 million.

11. The Nets were unable to keep Erving because they had to pay an additional $4.8 million to the Knicks upon their entry into the NBA on top of the $3.2 million expansion fee the four newcomers had to pay. The Nets tried to sell Erving to the Knicks in lieu of that fee, but the Knicks declined. Eventually, Erving went to the Philadelphia 76ers for $3 million.

12. Of the four teams who joined the NBA, the Spurs had the most immediate success with five division titles in their first six seasons. But it took until 1999 for them to become the first ABA team to win an NBA title.

13. After Gilmore went to the Bulls for $1.1 million for the first pick in the ABA dispersal draft, the next five players were selected from the Spirits of St. Louis for a combined $1.45 million.

14. According to Spurs owner Angelo Drossos, Celtics coach Red Auerbach was one of the most vocal opponents of the 3-point shot. That, of course, changed shortly after the Celtics drafted Larry Bird.

15. Moses Malone became the first player to bypass college and go straight to the pros when the Utah Stars selected him in the third round of the 1974 ABA draft.

TRIVIA TIME

1. Which of these teams did Larry Brown NOT serve as a head coach.

    A. The University of North Carolina
    B. San Antonio Spurs
    C. Detroit Pistons
    D. Kansas University

2. Who won the first slam dunk contest in 1976?

    A. David Thompson
    B. Larry Kenon
    C. Julius Erving
    D. Artis Gilmore

3. Who is the ABA's all-time leader in 3-point shooting percentage?

    A. Louie Dampier
    B. Darel Carrier
    C. Steve Jones
    D. Skeeter Swift

4. While Julius Erving is the only player to lead the ABA in scoring more than once, who set the all-time single-season scoring average at 34.6 points per game?

A. Rick Barry

B. Spencer Haywood

C. Dan Issel

D. Charlie Scott

5. Which of these nicknames did NOT belong to the Memphis ABA franchise from 1970-75?

A. Sounds

B. Jazz

C. Pros

D. Tams

ANSWERS:

1. A
2. C
3. B
4. D
5. B.

CHAPTER 3
HERE COME THE 1980S

The 1980s marked the beginning of the NBA's rise in popularity, which began to take off after Magic Johnson and Larry Bird carried their one-time rivalry in college in the 1979 NCAA Tournament championship game to the pros with the two most established teams in the NBA – Johnson to the Los Angeles Lakers and Bird to the Boston Celtics.

But that was almost scuttled before it took off. After the NBA had survived an external challenge in the form of an ABA, it now had a growing problem from within. A cocaine epidemic was sweeping through the league, and no one was sure how to combat it.

White Lines

While Grandmaster Flash's rap song "White Lines" didn't hit the airwaves until nearly a generation later in 1996, there was plenty of cocaine to go around in the 1980s in the NBA. A joint article written for the Washington Post and Los Angeles Times in the summer of 1980 surveyed people "in the game" who estimated that between 40 and 75 percent of players were using cocaine and one out of every 10 players were "free basing."

It was the drug of choice in the NBA and it cut across all player levels and lines. Jazz forward Bernard King was arrested for possession and faced an additional charge of sodomy at the time of his arrest. His teammate, Terry Furlow, died in a car accident. The autopsy revealed traces of cocaine and valium in his bloodstream.

At one point, Hawks president Stan Kasten estimated player use of cocaine at 75 percent, while team president Michael Gearon feared the league was on the verge of an epidemic of free base." Free base was a more dangerous way to do cocaine, but it also caused a stronger addiction due to the intense high it provided.

A 2013 book "Larceny Games" written by Brian Tuohy made the claim the 1981-82 Knicks team could have been shaving points and fixing games in conjunction with a drug dealer. That team had Micheal Ray Richardson, a talented yet troubled guard who was suspended by the league three times for drug use before being given a permanent ban by the NBA in 1986. The ban lasted all of two seasons.

In the latter part of the 1986-87 season, three Phoenix Suns players were indicted on charges of drug trafficking, and a fourth – team star Walter Davis – was suspended after having a relapse in his battle with cocaine.

But the cautionary tale for the 1980s cocaine epidemic in the

NBA was Len Bias. A talented forward at the University of Maryland, Bias was a two-time ACC Player of the Year and consensus first-team All-American in 1986. The Celtics selected him with the No. 2 overall pick that summer, with team president Red Auerbach having dreams of him and Larry Bird continuing Boston's dominance in the NBA.

But 48 hours after being selected, he returned to his dorm room and insufflated cocaine with friends and teammates in the overnight hours. He reportedly had a seizure and collapsed while talking with a friend. A 911 call made by a friend said Bias was "unconscious and not breathing." Less than three hours after that call, Bias was pronounced dead due to a cardiac arrhythmia related to the usage of cocaine.

The Celtics honored Bias with a memorial service, and the debate rages over whether or not Bias is the best player to never have played in the NBA.

Larry Legend Comes to Beantown Belatedly

Bird single-handedly carried little-known Indiana State to the NCAA title game in 1979. But even before that, the forward nicknamed "The Hick from French Lick" already had the NBA buzzing as one of its next potential stars.

Auerbach, the one-time Celtics coach responsible for their dynasty in the 1960s, had since moved into the front office and was determined to bring Bird to Boston. Auerbach was a master of scrutinizing every rule the league had and raised some eyebrows when he drafted Bird with the sixth pick in the 1978 draft.

Auerbach was legally allowed to do so since Bird was technically a member of the class of 1978. Many forget he started his collegiate career at Indiana, only to clash with Bobby Knight and leave Bloomington. It was after a short stint at Northwood Institute that he left for Terre Haute and Indiana State. Bird led the Sycamores to the 1978 NIT title, and with the Pacers holding the No. 1 pick that year, it made sense for Indiana to select the hometown hero.

But a meeting between Bird and Pacers GM Bob Leonard convinced the latter it might not be the best idea to draft Bird, who wanted to stay in college and could also demand a high salary if he did decide to come out and play in the pros. Eventually, Indiana traded the pick to Portland for the No. 3 selection and guard Johnny Davis.

And with Bird and the Sycamores going 33-0 before losing to Johnson and the Spartans, Auerbach looked like a genius yet again for his stashed draft pick.

Magic Casts a Spell in La-La Land

Their fates already entwined by the most-watched televised college basketball game, Earvin "Magic" Johnson did not have the same drama surrounding his lead-in to being drafted. The newly anointed NCAA Tournament champ was the first overall pick in the 1979 draft after averaging 17.1 points, 7.9 assists and 7.6 rebounds.

The 6-foot-9 Johnson revolutionized the point guard position because of his size and ball-handling skills. He could run the break, operate in the low post as a scorer, run a half-court offense and play some decent defense. No one since Oscar Robertson had the same skill-set as Magic Johnson, and it would take until LeBron James to see it again.

Johnson had instant success in the NBA, helped in large part by the presence of Kareem Abdul-Jabbar. But it was in Abdul-Jabbar's absence in which Johnson started writing his legend as a pro. He filled in at center for the injured 7-foot-2 star and finished with 42 points, 15 rebounds and seven assists as the Lakers defeated Julius Erving and the Philadelphia 76ers 123-107 to win the NBA title.

A Skyline is Built in Houston

Size has long been coveted in the NBA, where a 7-footer can make a difference in a whole host of areas. But what if you had two 7-footers? Could you play them at the same time and not sacrifice speed against quicker teams? Could they co-exist on offense taking up that much space in the low post?

In 1983, the Rockets drafted 7-foot-4 Ralph Sampson, who had been a three-time All-American and three-time ACC Player of the Year at Virginia. Because there was still no NBA Draft lottery, the Rockets won the top overall pick by virtue of a coin flip. The year before, Sampson opted against entering the draft because the San Diego Clippers potentially could have won the No. 1 selection.

The Rockets made only marginal gains in Sampson's rookie season, more than doubling their win total while still finishing a horrid 29-53. Unlike Sampson, Olajuwon was able to take a leap of faith on the draft coin flip since the options were Houston, where he played collegiately as part of the great "Phi Slamma Jamma" teams of Guy Lewis or Portland. The Rockets won the coin toss and made Olajuwon the No. 1 overall pick, two ahead of the Chicago Bulls, who selected a guard from North Carolina named Michael Jordan.

The two 7-footers instantly transformed the Rockets, making them instant contenders in the Western Conference. Olajuwon, a relentless learner who spent summers learning under the tutelage of one-time Rockets center Moses Malone, had the low-post finesse that perfectly complemented Sampson's classic back-to-the-basket game.

The Rockets improved another 19 games that year and made the playoffs, losing to the Jazz in the first round. But the 1985-86 season was one to remember as the Rockets won the Midwest Division and thrashed the Lakers in five games in the Western Conference finals. However, Bird and the 67-win Celtics were waiting in the finals and disposed of the Rockets in six games.

The "Twin Towers" experiment ended midway through the next season, when Sampson had a falling out with coach Bill Fitch and was traded to Golden State as part of a four-player deal.

Michael Jeffrey Jordan – The Early Years

Much has always been made about the fact Jordan "lasted" until the third overall pick in 1984, but Olajuwon created a Hall of Fame worthy career for himself while with the Rockets. And in the case of the Trail Blazers selecting Sam Bowie, well Jordan would have been a surplus of needs since they already had a pretty good shooting guard of their own in Clyde Drexler. Another Hall of Famer.

So Jordan essentially fell into the Bulls' laps at No. 3. But it still took some time for the greatest guard of his generation and arguably of all time to learn how to win. Remember, Jordan had no perimeter game early in his career. He averaged 28.2 points as a rookie while going just 9 for 52 from beyond the arc in the 1984-85 season.

That team finished 38-44 and was sent packing in the first round of the playoffs. He missed all but 18 games of his second season due to a foot injury, but served notice of his burgeoning star power when he averaged 43.7 points in a three-game sweep at the hands of the Celtics. His 63-point effort in a 135-131 double-overtime loss set a playoff scoring record that still stands.

Jordan's first winning season in Chicago did not come until the Bulls went 50-32 in 1987-88 and finished second to the Detroit Pistons, who would fluster him as he entered the prime of the first act of his career.

Motown's "Bad Boys"

Speaking of those Pistons, they supplanted the Celtics as the East's best team in the late 1980s after having gone through the rites of passage by being beat by the Celtics earlier in the decade. Coach Chuck Daly had assembled a strong nine-man rotation that featured stars in Isiah Thomas and Adrian Dantley as well as a rough-and-tumble frontcourt paced by Bill Laimbeer and a gangly youngster named Dennis Rodman.

While the nickname "Bad Boys" came about by way of a copy editor naming Detroit's 1987-88 season highlights tape with that title, the Pistons were a team that played fullcourt defense with gusto. Nothing was conceded, and disruption was the name of their game. Bumps were frequent, elbows were common and the swagger the Pistons carried was both hated and envied throughout the league. The Pistons nearly broke through in 1987, but lost in the conference finals to the Celtics in seven games as the home team won every time.

This was also the series that cemented the Pistons' "Bad Boys" persona as enraged Celtics center Robert Parrish suddenly pummeled Laimbeer late in Game 5. It turned out to be payback for a hard foul Laimbeer landed on Bird two games prior that almost started a brawl and got both players ejected, but the sight of the quiet Parish unloading a forearm to the face of Laimbeer as the two battled for a rebound showed how much antagonism existed between the teams.

Detroit would break through the next season for the first of its three straight NBA Finals appearances, falling to the Lakers in seven games. But the Pistons would win the next two titles, setting the tone of physical play that would permeate throughout the Eastern Conference in the 1990s.

The NBA Draft Lottery

After the Rockets selected Olajuwon with the first pick in 1984, there continued to be outcry that teams were tanking to make sure they could be one of the top two picks and part of the coin flip to determine who won the No. 1 overall pick. Commissioner David Stern then changed the method of the draft order to a full-fledged lottery in which every non-playoff team had an equal chance of securing the No. 1 overall pick.

The 1985 draft turned into great theater since Georgetown center Patrick Ewing was clearly the best player available to be selected and would be a cornerstone in any franchise. The event instantly became must-see television for all NBA fans, and the conspiracy theorists of sport instantly cried foul when the New York Knicks won the first draft lottery and selected Ewing. From frozen envelopes to dented corners of envelopes, there are still people who believe the first NBA draft lottery was rigged to help the team in the biggest media market.

Since then, the NBA has come up with tweaks to protect teams with the worst record from falling too far down the draft board since there are now 14 non-playoff teams every year. But it sometimes can't be helped when these struggling teams trade away picks years in advance and it winds up with good teams having the top pick... like the Boston Celtics do this summer after reaching the Eastern Conference finals.

Cleveland... still a mistake by the lake

There was little good news in the world of sports in Cleveland in the 1980s – the Indians never finished above fifth place the entire decade, the Browns lost to the Broncos three times in a four-year span in the AFC title game, but the Cavaliers were their own unique brand of futility tanks to the ineptitude of owner Ted Stepien.

From the 1980-81 through the 1983-84 seasons, the Cavaliers never won more than 28 games, in large part due to Stepien's bumbling. He alienated the community with disparaging remarks against the African-American community and was vilified by the team's remaining fans when he ran play-by-play announcer Joe Tait out of town.

But what set Stepien apart from other meddlesome owners was

the team's propensity to trade away first-round picks. In the two-plus seasons Stepien owned the team from 1980-82, the Cavaliers dealt five first-round picks, including three to the expansion Dallas Mavericks. It got to the point where the league had to step in and pass what became known as the "Stepien Rule" in which restricted teams from trading first-round picks in consecutive years.

And those decisions crippled the franchise for more than a decade. They dealt away their top pick in 1982, which turned out to be the No. 1 pick overall. The Lakers used that on James Worthy. The following year, the Mavericks took Derek Harper with the 11th overall pick they acquired from Cleveland.

In 1984, the Cavs would have had the fourth overall pick, which the Mavericks used on Sam Perkins. Other options that year included Auburn forward Charles Barkley and Gonzaga point guard John Stockton. The Cavaliers selected center Tim McCormick 12th that year, a compensation pick provided by the league to help overcome Stepien's mistakes, but they promptly dealt him to Seattle.

His last deal with the Mavericks that gave Dallas a first-round pick in 1986 turned out to be center Roy Tarpley.

The Nuggets' Talented Trio

While the Lakers and Rockets dominated the headlines in the early 1980s, there were some other good teams in the Western

Conference. One was the Denver Nuggets, coached by Doug Moe. The former ABA guard developed a high-tempo offense that didn't seem to operate on any set of principles aside from moving the ball quickly and shoot even quicker.

It also helped Moe had three standout players in Dan Issel, Alex English and Kiki Vandeweghe. Issel, nicknamed "The Horse" for his durability, was a holdover from the ABA days and could still score with anyone regardless of league. The ABA's all-time leading scorer averaged at least 21.6 points in five straight seasons for the Nuggets while making the playoffs every year.

English was originally a second-round pick by the Bucks in 1976 and didn't blossom until the Nuggets acquired him in a trade from Indiana during the 1979-80 season. He averaged at least 23.8 points in his next nine seasons in Denver, earning honors as the top scorer in the NBA for the 1980s, and his 25,613 career points rank 17th all-time.

VanDeWeghe was originally selected 11th by the Mavericks in 1980, but forced a trade to Denver by December. His three full seasons with the Nuggets were incredibly proficient as he averaged 21.5, 26.7 and 29.4 points. His career high of 51 points came in the NBA's highest-scoring game of all-time, a 186-184 triple-overtime loss to the Detroit Pistons.

In a three-season stretch from 1981-84, the Nuggets averaged 124.5 points behind the trio. However, their lack of defense meant they also allowed 124.5 points per game as they outscored opponents by just four points over those 246 contests while going 129-117.

The Woeful San Diego Clippers

Despite his best efforts, Stepien did not have a monopoly on ineptitude at the ownership level. While Donald Sterling gained worldwide notoriety for his racist comments in 2014, he was sowing the seeds of misery in the Clippers franchise as a fledgling owner in the 1980s. He bought the team in 1981 for the paltry sum of $12.5 million with promises of making the team into a contender.

You couldn't go anywhere in San Diego without seeing Sterling's face on a bus or a billboard. But while his friend Jerry Buss instantly turned the Lakers into a contender, Sterling was left with a sagging Clippers franchise that didn't have a winning record throughout the decade.

The NBA fined him when he publicly said it would be OK if his team would finish last for a better chance to select Sampson with the first pick in the 1983 draft. His love affair with moving the team to Los Angeles began in 1982, and an investigation by his fellow owners resulted in a recommendation to terminate him as an owner due to late payments to creditors and players.

But the following year, then-vice president David Stern suggested to Sterling he let Alan Rothenberg – the eventual savior of soccer in the United States – to take over the day-today duties of the team. Sterling relented, and the palace coup wouldn't take place for another three decades.

RANDOM FACTS AND FIGURES

1. The 1985-86 Bulls finished 30-52 and still qualified for the playoffs. It remains the worst postseason qualifying record in NBA history.

2. Jordan's 63-point game stands out for a few reasons. One is that he didn't attempt a 3-pointer. In fact, the Bulls only took two in 102 shots for the game. Two is that Jordan was a very good free throw shooter. He sank 19 of 21 from the line in that game. And third, despite taking 41 shots from the field, he also led the team with six assists.

3. The Lakers' Game 7 victory in 1988 was their first in the finals since moving to Los Angeles in 1960. They had lost the previous five decisive games since winning the title in 1954 while located in Minneapolis.

4. In VanDeWeghe's 51-point game, he combined with English and Issel for 126 of the team's 184 points on 50 of 78 shooting. The Pistons had a potent trio of their own as Thomas, Kelly Tripucka and John Long accounted for 123 points while making 50 of 84 shots from the field. The game was tied at 145 at the end of regulation.

5. Magic Johnson far and away had the most assists in the 1980s with 8,369. Thomas was a distant second with 6,985.

6. Like Jordan, it took some time for Ewing to have a winning season. The Knicks won only 47 games in his first two seasons and then made the playoffs in 1988 despite finish 38-44. They finally broke through the following season, the second and last under Rick Pitino, going 52-30 and reaching the second round before Pitino left to resurrect the University of Kentucky.

7. For all of Bird's prowess from 3-point range, the Celtics never used it as a primary weapon. Bird finished sixth in the 1980s with 462 3-pointers made – even one-time teammate Danny Ainge had more (514).

8. Philadelphia 76ers guard Maurice Cheeks had nearly as many defensive rebounds (1,731) as he did steals (1,709) in the 1980s.

9. Jordan finished 15th in points scored in the 1980s with 14,016 despite playing only 427 games. Every other player in the top 25 in scoring played at least 597 games.

10. All told, six players were given one-year bans for cocaine use in the 1980s. They were: John Drew, Micheal Ray Richardson, Lewis Lloyd, Mitchell Wiggins, Duane Washington and Chris Washburn. Richardson, Wiggins and Washburn were all first-round picks, and Richardson and Washburn went fourth and third overall, respectively.

11. It may be one of the closest things to an unassailable record

in NBA history – Magic Johnson has 2,346 postseason assists, 507 more than second-place John Stockton. Heading into the 2017 NBA Finals, LeBron James is third with 1,439.

12. Five different players had 60-point games in the 1980s, paced by Jordan's 69. The others were Karl Malone, Bird, Tom Chambers and Bernard King.

13. There continues to be debate over whether Thomas "froze out" Jordan during the 1985 All-Star game. It was Jordan's first All-Star game and veteran players were reportedly upset over Jordan's flashy ways. While both Jordan and Thomas downplayed the talk, Johnson said it did happen in a book he co-wrote with Bird and Jackie MacMullan called "When the Game was Ours."

14. How bad were the Clippers in the 1980s? Despite losing in the 1987 NBA Finals, the Celtics still had more wins that postseason (13) than the Clippers did in the 1986-87 regular season (12).

15. David Robinson didn't arrive in San Antonio until the 1989-90 season, but his impact was instant. The Spurs improved 35 games in the win column from 21 to 56 and won their first Division title since 1983.

TRIVIA TIME

1. How many NBA Finals appearances did the Lakers make from 1980-81 to 1989-90?

   A. 5

   B. 7

   C. 6

   D. 8

2. Adrian Dantley ended his playing career in which team?

   A. Buffalo Braves

   B. Utah Jazz

   C. Milwaukee Bucks

   D. Detroit Pistons

3. True or False: The Boston Celtics won at least 50 games every season during the 1980s?

4. Because of the Celtics and the 76ers, the Milwaukee Bucks were one of the best Eastern Conference teams of the 1980s no one remembers. How many consecutive Central Division titles did they win that decade?

   A. 3

   B. 5

   C. 4

   D. 6

5. In 1980-81, the expansion Dallas Mavericks began their first NBA season. Who was their leading average scorer?

A. Brad Davis

B. Jim Spanarkel

C. Geoff Huston

D. Tom LaGarde

ANSWERS:

1. B
2. C
3. False, the Celtics went 42-40 in 1988-89.
4. D
5. C.

CHAPTER 4

THE 1990S AND THE RUNNING OF THE BULLS

They won six titles with him and nearly a seventh when he cut his comeback short after less than two seasons. They are the closest thing to a dynasty the NBA has had since the Celtics teams of the 1960s. Beloved in Chicago and hated by nearly everyone else (though that occasionally included some of his teammates), Michael Jordan brought the NBA to the next level when Larry Bird and Magic Johnson could no longer go on.

Michel Jeffrey Jordan, the Prime Years (1991-93)

While Jordan was tearing the league apart and averaging better than 30 points per game, he still had not been to an NBA Finals entering his seventh season in the league. Two conference finals losses to the eventual NBA champion Detroit Pistons only fueled his rage to get to the top of the heap.

Jordan's scoring prowess continued unabated in the postseason during Chicago's first three-peat as he averaged 33.7 points in

58 playoff games. He was held under 20 just once in that span and had 11 40-point games. Five of those 40-point games came in the NBA Finals, including a 55-point effort in a Game 4 win.

Jordan had two iconic moments during those three titles, the first his famous switch of hand on a drive to finish a layup In Game 2 against the Los Angeles Lakers in 1991. People remember the drive before the fact he had 33 points and 13 assists in just 36 minutes while shooting 15 of 18.

The second was the shrug as he torched the Portland Trail Blazers for six straight 3-pointers as part of a 35-point first half that set a Finals record in 1992. For his career including the playoffs, Jordan made six or more 3-pointers just four times in 1,251 games.

John Tesh's lasting contribution to the NBA

Depending on your age, you know John Tesh as the co-host of "Entertainment Tonight" with Mary Hart, the husband of actress Connie Selleca or for the Twitter age, someone who offers life hacks to better your everyday existence. However, to NBA fans, he is the composer of "Roundball Rock," which served as the NBA on NBC theme song from 1990-2002.

As he once recounted at a concert, Tesh came up with the melody and called his home answering machine to leave the message with a beat-box melody as a reminder to continue composing the melody. It is estimated NBC played "Roundball

Rock" in excess of 12,000 times.

Clyde the Glide Finally Gets a Ring

After the 1992 loss to the Bulls, time was against Clyde Drexler for winning an NBA title. The Trail Blazers had gradually fallen out of contention in the following years, and in 1995, Drexler asked the organization to trade him to a contender. His hometown of Houston answered Portland's call as the Rockets acquired him before the trade deadline for Otis Thorpe.

Drexler spent the 35 games after the deal learning how to play with Hakeem Olajuwon once more. It was a reunion of the "Phi Slamma Jamma" days when they were teammates at the University of Houston. The Rockets finished sixth in the West and needed the maximum 12 games to get past Utah and Phoenix in the first two rounds.

The Rockets returned to the NBA Finals to defend their title against the Orlando Magic, who handed Jordan his only series loss in the seven years bridging his titles. The veteran duo of Olajuwon and Drexler proved too much for burgeoning stars Shaquille O'Neal and Anfernee Hardaway as Houston swept Orlando to repeat as NBA champions.

Penny and Lil' Penny

While O'Neal and Hardaway were teammates, they belonged to rival sneaker companies. O'Neal was the primary pitchman for

Reebok and Hardaway was being touted by Nike. The soft-spoken Hardaway was a perfect foil to the loquacious O'Neal, and Nike executives came up with the concept of Lil' Penny, a talking doll who doubled as Hardaway's alter ego.

The list of rumored voices to be Lil Penny carried almost as much star power in Hollywood as the NBA. Eddie Murphy. Damon Wayans. Martin Lawrence. All three were reportedly considered for the commercial spots before it was given to Chris Rock, who was an up-and-coming comic on Saturday Night Live and In Living Color.

Rock and Hardaway hit it off instantly and the result was a two-year Nike campaign that turned Hardaway into a star and vaulted Rock to superstardom. But the commercials were also so successful that it also became the first wedge to come between Hardaway and O'Neal that led to the latter's eventual departure to Los Angeles.

The Admiral Sinks Shaq

By all accounts, David Robinson was considered one of the most giving players in the NBA. A community standout and Naval Academy graduate, Robinson had the perfect landing place in San Antonio, a city long known for its excellent working relationship with the U.S. military. So it's not surprising that the one time Robinson decided to be selfish, everyone rooted for him.

Heading into the final game of the season, Robinson trailed

O'Neal by .06 points in the scoring race. Spurs coach John Lucas wanted Robinson to win the title, so all of San Antonio's offense was going to go through the 7-foot center. Despite being double, triple and sometimes quadruple-teamed, Robinson ended with a franchise-record 71 points. While purists often complain about how the Spurs were fouling the Clippers to get the ball back for the offense, Robinson did hit 26 of 41 shots from the field and 18 of 25 free throws.

The result left O'Neal needing 68 points to retake the lead from Robinson in his finale versus the New Jersey Nets. He finished with 32, and Robinson joined George Gervin as the only Spurs to win scoring titles.

Petrovic's Passing

Though Jordan was the dominant force in the NBA, there was a time where the New Jersey Nets were on the verge of creating a legitimate rivalry with their crosstown neighbors, the New York Knicks. And that was in large part due to Drazen Petrovic.

A native Croatian, Petrovic was well-known in international circles and had won three Olympic medals. Seeking a bigger challenge after dominating at the club level in Europe, Petrovic came across the Atlantic to play in the NBA. His first season-plus with Portland, which owned his rights as a third-round pick in 1986, was unremarkable, but a midseason trade to New Jersey changed everything.

The Nets cleared out the shooting guard position for Petrovic to start in the 1991-92 season, and he formed a potent tandem with forward Derrick Coleman, averaging 20.6 points and helping New Jersey make the playoffs. He averaged 22.3 points the following season and was a third-team all-NBA selection.

However, Petrovic's life was tragically cut short at the age of 28 in a car accident. But he is always remembered as one of the first European guards to make an impact in the NBA.

Webber makes history, in a good way

Chris Webber was already guaranteed not to be forgotten for his ill-fated timeout call in the 1993 NCAA Tournament final against North Carolina. But the most famous member of Michigan's "Fab 5" would be the answer to another trivia question before playing his first NBA minute.

Orlando held the first pick in the 1993 draft and was putting together a team around O'Neal. Golden State was sitting at No. 3, and coach Don Nelson was looking for a frontcourt player to bolster his undersized team. The two worked out a draft-and-trade arrangement in which the Magic selected Webber and the Warriors picked Hardaway before the two teams traded the players straight up.

It was the first time a No. 1 pick was ever dealt on draft day, though one could argue Hardaway and the Magic got the better of the deal since they made the NBA Finals in Hardaway's second season. Webber, meanwhile, only came as close as the conference finals on two occasions.

The pre-cursor to LeBron

Before LeBron was considered to be the perfect basketball player in terms of size and skill, there was Grant Hill. The son of former Dallas Cowboys wide receiver Calvin Hill, the younger Hill enjoyed a standout career at Duke, winning back-to-back NCAA Tournament titles while becoming the first ACC Player to total 1,900 points, 700 rebounds, 400 assists, 200 steals and 100 blocks.

Hill was the third overall pick in the 1994 draft behind Glenn Robinson and Jason Kidd, but his first six seasons compare favorably against almost anyone at his position. He averaged 21.6 points, 7.9 rebounds and 6.3 assists in that span before injuries took their toll. Hill also recorded all of his 29 triple-doubles with the Pistons.

Over the remaining 12 seasons, Hill never reached the 20-point mark and played more than 70 games just three times. He never got out of the first round of the playoffs with Detroit, and almost half of his playoff career came with Phoenix in 2010 when the Suns reached the conference finals.

The short-lived life of Run TMC

While none of them failed from Hollis, Queens, there was no act in basketball like Tim Hardaway, Mitch Richmond and Chris Mullin in Golden State for the 1989-90 and 1990-91 seasons. The sharp-shooting trio, which gained the moniker "Run TMC" combined to average 72.7 points in 1990-91 as the Warriors scored 116.6 per game.

Mullin was the leader of the three, the Brooklyn native and small forward averaging 25.7 points while shooting 53.6 percent. He scored in double figures in all 82 games and scored 30 or more 21 times.

Hardaway had a nickname before joining "Run TMC" from his college playing days. The point guard had a devastating crossover that was dubbed "The UTEP two-step" while playing at Texas-El Paso under legendary coach Don Haskins. But Hardaway was the designated perimeter threat and hit a team-high 97 3-pointers.

Richmond was the last member to join as the fifth overall pick in the 1988 draft by the Warriors from Kansas State. He was a volume scorer throughout his career, averaging 21.9 points or better his first 10 seasons in the league.

In their final 127 games together, all three players scored at least 20 points in the same game 48 times. But for all their proficiency, it failed to translate into postseason success. The Warriors didn't make the playoffs in 1990 and then lost in the second round in 1991.

An Unlikely Trio

Jordan's 27 games in his 1995 comeback served as the rust scraping for his second act. While Pippen continued to be his running partner, general manager Jerry Krause rebuilt the team around them, most notably with Toni Kukoc.

Kukoc earned a special place in Bulls lore because both Jordan and Pippen loathed him at first. Krause was convinced Kukoc was going to be a star when he selected him in the second round of the 1990 draft. While Jordan and Krause rarely saw eye to eye, Krause enraged Pippen during a contract squabble as he was trying to save cap space for the Croatian.

In a group play game at the 1992 Olympics, Jordan and Pippen thoroughly manhandled Kukoc, limiting him to four points as the U.S. blasted Croatia by 33 points. After the game, Pippen said, "Now I guess (the Bulls) see he's not ready for prime-time competition."

But by the time Jordan's second go-round started, Kukoc was an established sixth man with the Bulls. He averaged 13 points in each of those three title-winning seasons as part of a 13-year career that also made stops in Philadelphia, Atlanta and Milwaukee minus the fanfare of being hounded by Jordan and Pippen.

RANDOM FACTS AND FIGURES

1. In the Bulls first "three-peat" from 1990-93, they lost 13 postseason games. But seven came in 1992 after they posted a 67-15 mark, the best record of those three title-winning teams.

2. In their 72-win 1995-96 season, the Bulls lost nine of their 10 games by a combined 45 points. The other was a 32-point pummeling by the Knicks. Jordan had 32 points in that game but the rest of the team combined for 40 on 16 of 50 shooting in that 104-72 loss.

3. Cavaliers guard Mark Price was the only player to shoot better than 90 percent from the foul line in the 1990s, converting 91.9 percent. He missed 110 free throws in eight seasons.

4. By comparison, Shaquille O'Neal missed a staggering 2,524 free throws while converting 53.4 percent of them in eight seasons after entering the NBA in 1992. If he made even half of those misses, he would have topped 30,000 points for his career.

5. The 3-pointer was far more embraced in the 1990s than in the 1980s, with 13 players making at least 1,000 shots from beyond the arc. Pacers guard Reggie Miller led the charge

with 1,558 makes.

6. Despite the increase of 3-point shooters, there were more proficient scorers in the 1980s. Only 33 players scored 10,000 or more points in the 1990s compared to 44 in the 1980s.

7. Of those 71 players who accomplished scoring 10,000 in each of those two decades, only five did it in both the 1980s and 1990s: Jordan, Hakeem Olajuwon, Clyde Drexler, Charles Barkley and Karl Malone.

8. He may have been crazy, but Dennis Rodman was crazy good at getting rebounds. His 9,343 caroms collected during the 1990s was nearly one thousand more than Dikembe Mutombo, who was second with 8,439 in one less season.

9. Because of the Bulls, there were some very good teams to never win an NBA title. Five of their six titles came against 60-win teams from the Western Conference, with both the 1995-96 Seattle and the 1996-97 Utah teams going 64-18. The 1990-91 Portland squad went 63-19, while the 1992-93 Phoenix and 1997-98 Utah teams were both 62-20.

10. Though the Clippers did finally achieve a winning season for owner Donald Sterling by going 45-37 in the 1991-92 campaign, it would be their only one over .500 until going 47-35 in the 2005-06 season.

11. Scottie Pippen played a staggering 156 playoff games in the 1990s, the equivalent of nearly two full seasons. Jazz teammates John Stockton and Karl Malone are tied for a distant second with 130.

12. Miller's 3-point shooting percentages in the regular season and the postseason during the 1990s were both 40.5 percent.

13. From 1991-98, Charles Barkley was whistled for at least 22 technical fouls in every season, with a high-water mark of 32 over just 66 games in the 1994-95 season.

14. Only three players blocked at least 300 shots in a season during the 1990s: Olajuwon, Mutombo and David Robinson.

15. Stockton is one of only three players to record 1,000 assists in a season. He did it four times in the 1990s, setting the NBA record with 1,164 in 1990-91.

TRIVIA TIME

1. How many times did Michael Jordan lead the NBA in scoring during the 1990s?

    A. 8

    B. 6

    C. 7

    D. 9

2. Which of these nicknames did Shaquille O'Neal NOT give himself?

    A. The Big Aristotle

    B. Wilt Chamberneezy

    C. The Geaux Tiger

    D. Shaq Fu

3. Lionel Simmons played his last professional game of basketball in NBA in which year?

    A. 1991

    B. 1995

    C. 1997

    D. 2000

4. Which Duke player was the only overall No. 1 pick in the NBA Draft during the 1990s?

    A. Grant Hill

    B. Christian Laettner

C. Elton Brand

D. Bobby Hurley

5. How many points did San Antonio Spurs center David Robinson score in the final game of the 1993-94 season to win the NBA scoring title?

A. 47

B. 62

C. 71

D. 58

ANSWERS:

1. B
2. C
3. C
4. C
5. C

CHAPTER 5

THE 2000S AND THE RISE
OF THE SUPER TEAMS

The first decade of the 21st century is always going to be remembered as the one that gave the NBA superstars LeBron James, Dwyane Wade and Carmelo Anthony in the top-heavy class of 2003, but one of the other things that began to materialize was the formation of super teams as clubs figured out creative ways to work stars under the salary cap.

About that 2003 draft class

Let's face it, if it wasn't for Darko Milicic going No. 2 to the Detroit Pistons, this could have been the top five of any draft class in NBA history. James, Wade and No. 4 overall pick Chris Bosh all won a title together and Anthony is arguably one of the best offensive players of this generation who simply never found postseason success.

But Milicic deserves special mention for just how much of a bust he is. The native of Yugoslavia never averaged more than 8.8 points in any season and that didn't come until his eighth one while with Minnesota in 2010-11. It took him five seasons to be a full-time starter, and the 7-footer finished with 29 career double-doubles, a total James eclipsed midway through his second season.

Oooh La La

Not much was expected of Tony Parker when he was drafted by the Spurs in 2001. He considered attending UCLA after a standout game at the Nike Hoop Summit, but he opted to return to France and play in the domestic professional league.

Parker failed to help himself at a pre-draft workout with the Spurs. Under the vigilant eye of Coach Gregg Popovich, Parker was manhandled by Lance Blanks, whose biggest claim to fame was being part of the "BMW" set of guards at the University of Texas. After a short while, Popovich debated whether Parker should even stay at the summer camp, but invited him back for a second workout.

Popovich then sweated out draft day and finally was able to select Parker with the 28th overall pick. More than 18,500 points and four NBA titles later, the point guard was as an integral part of San Antonio's rise to dominance as Tim Duncan.

Super Team 1.0

While teams in the late 2000s and beyond were able to create "Big 3" combinations that turned them into instant NBA title contenders, the first team to really try this after the turn of the century was the 2003-04 Lakers.

A team that had championship cornerstones in Kobe Bryant and Shaquille O'Neal – the pair won three straight titles from 2000-02 – added aging veteran superstars Gary Payton and Karl Malone. Both players and future Hall of Famers had lost in previous NBA Finals during Jordan's reign of dominance in the 1990s and went all in.

But the quartet, who had combined for 86,262 points heading into the 2003-04 season, were denied what would have been the Lakers' fourth NBA title in five years as they lost to the Pistons in five games. It would be Malone's last season in the league, while Payton eventually got his ring two years later with Miami.

The True Star of the North

Both the Vancouver Grizzlies and Toronto Raptors joined the NBA in 1995, but by 2001, the Grizzlies had relocated to Memphis and left the Raptors as Canada's only franchise. The left the weight of a nation on the shoulders of high-flying Vince Carter.

Carter was the fifth overall pick in 1998 by the Warriors, who traded him to the Raptors for North Carolina teammate Antawn Jamison, the No. 4 overall pick. Even with the lockout shortening his rookie season to 50 games, the 27 losses exceeded his entire total in three seasons with the Tar Heels.

While Raptors fans never warmed to the 2000 Slam Dunk

champion, he did help the team to its first three playoff appearances in franchise history and first playoff series win in 2001 when they defeated the Knicks in five games.

Rip and Ray

Both were standout players at Connecticut and top-notch offensive players with different styles. One was a slashing, driving player with an excellent mid-range games and the other a three-point specialist who was one of the best in NBA history. And both Richard Hamilton and Ray Allen were NBA champions.

Hamilton was originally the seventh overall pick in 1999 by the Washington Wizards, but he was shipped to Detroit as part of a six-player deal that included Jerry Stackhouse. Hamilton blossomed with the Pistons, averaging at least 17.3 points in each of his eight seasons in Motown. He scored 21.5 points per game in helping the Pistons beat the Lakers in five games for their first NBA title since 1990.

Allen was the fifth overall pick by the Minnesota Timberwolves in 1996 and was shipped to Milwaukee in a draft-day deal for Stephon Marbury. His 3-point skills were lethal — he made at least 100 3-pointers in every season except the lockout-shortened 1999-2000 campaign.

Allen nearly got the Bucks into the NBA Finals for the first time since 1974 as they lost in seven games to the 76ers in 2001, and never found a good supporting cast in Seattle. When he arrived in Boston for the 2007-08, he became part of the first "Big 3" with Paul Pierce and Kevin Garnett. The trio won an NBA title in 2008, and Allen won a second title in 2013 with the Heat.

Dirk Does Dallas

The last 30 years have seen an impressive influx of foreign players enter the NBA to make it a truly global game. And while Rockets center Yao Ming will get the most credit for changing the culture of the league in making it a worldwide sport, the best international player in this era could very well be Dirk Nowitzki.

The 7-foot German originally lasted until the ninth selection in 1998, when the Milwaukee Bucks picked him. But they traded his rights to the Mavericks for Robert Traylor, who was taken sixth. Traylor's career could be labeled a bust as he averaged 4.8 points and 3.7 rebounds, Nowitzki finished the 2016-17 ranked sixth all-time in points (30,260), 14th in 3-pointers made (1,780) and 29th in rebounds (10,893).

A 13-time All-Star, Nowitzki led the Mavericks to their only title in franchise history as they beat the Miami Heat in six games in 2011. Traylor, meanwhile, played 22 postseason games and only made it past the first round in 2002 with the Charlotte Hornets.

Allen Iverson, the one-man gang

Allen Iverson averaged 30 or more points four times during the 2000s, but what made it impressive is that in three of those seasons, he had next to no one to lighten the load offensively.

He averaged 31.1 points in leading the 76ers to the 2001 NBA Finals, the next-highest scorer was Theo Ratliff (12.4 ppg). The following season he scored 31.4 per game, and Derrick Coleman was runner-up at 15.8 per contest. In 2004-05, Iverson netted 30.7 per contest, and late-season acquisition Chris Webber finished second by averaging 15.6 points in 21 games. The next season, Webber flourished as a legitimate No. 2 option and averaged 20.2 points while Iverson posted 33 per game.

Aside from their run to the 2001 NBA Finals, Iverson's rampant scoring skills went wasted. In those other three aforementioned seasons, the Sixers lost in the first round of the playoffs twice and failed to qualify in 2005-06.

Points Aplenty in 2005-06

Kobe Bryant's 35.4 points per game in 2005-06 was the highest average in the NBA since Jordan had 37.09 in 1986-87. But the 2005-06 campaign also marked the first time since 1981-82 that the league's top three scorers all averaged at least 30 points.

Chasing Bryant that season was Iverson (33.01) and James (31.37), while the 1981-82 leaderboard was headed by George Gervin (32.29), Moses Malone (31.11) and Adrian Dantley (30.33).

Washington's Gilbert Arenas narrowly missed the 30-point mark as well, falling 54 points short. Had that happened, it would have been the first time the NBA had four players averaging 30 points since Wilt Chamberlain, Walt Bellamy, Bob Pettit, Jerry West and Oscar Robertson all averaged 30.8 points or better in 1961-62.

A Hello to Durant and a Farewell to Seattle

At the end of the 2007-08 season, the SuperSonics franchise moved to Oklahoma City, which also marked the rookie season of 19-year-old Kevin Durant. The second overall pick of the 2007 draft averaged 20.3 points – still the lowest mark of his 10-year career – as Seattle won just 20 games.

It was a sad end for a team that had gotten to the 1996 NBA Finals. Seattle had made the playoffs just twice in its final seven seasons in the Emerald City and won 86 games combined in the last three.

Considering how the Thunder drafted Russell Westbrook in their first season in Oklahoma City, one could only imagine Seattle fans watching Durant and Westbrook the way they did Gary Payton and Shawn Kemp a decade earlier.

Shaq's Ring Chasing

O'Neal's three championships with the Lakers also resulted in him winning the NBA Finals MVP award three times. But the "Big Aristotle" turned into the "Big Mercenary" in the later part of the decade as he tried to add more titles to his already glittering resume.

He was first dealt from the Lakers to the Heat prior to the 2004-05 season and played the key supporting role in Miami's 2006 title with Dwyane Wade. Then he was dealt to Phoenix before the 2008 trade deadline for Shawn Marion, but little came from that as the Suns lost in the first round that year.

Prior to the 2009-10 season, Phoenix shipped him to Cleveland in a three-player deal. That was arguably his best chance to win a fifth ring as the Cavaliers won the Central and were the top seed in the East, but they were upset in the conference semifinals by Boston.

Sensing something could be in Boston, O'Neal signed as a free agent there before the 2010-11 season. He was limited to 37 games due to a series of leg injuries and played just 12 minutes over two games in the playoffs as Wade and the Heat eliminated the Cavaliers in the second round.

After winning his last title in 2006, O'Neal appeared in just 22 playoff games and averaged 12.7 points while his teams went 8-14. He had averaged 25.6 points in 194 prior postseason games while compiling a 121-73 mark.

RANDOM FACTS AND FIGURES

1. San Antonio Spurs forward Tim Duncan had two triple-doubles and 20 double-doubles in 24 postseason games en route to the 2003 NBA title. He had 28 and 8 and 36 and 9 in the two games he failed to notch at least a double-double.

2. Both Michael Redd and Rasheed Wallace finished one 3-pointer shy of making 1,000 for the first decade of the 21st century.

3. Unlike the 1990s, three players shot 90 percent or better from the foul line in the 2000s. Though he was there for only five seasons, Reggie Miller shot 91.5 percent and missed just 114 free throws. Steve Nash and Ray Allen, both of whom played the entire decade, shot 90.8 and 90.3 percent, respectively and sank a combined 5,135 of 5,673 from the charity stripe.

4. Three of the top 10 players in shooting percentage in the 2000s were foreign-born as Brazilian Nene Hilario was third (55.4 percent), China's Yao Ming was eighth (52.5) and Spain's Pau Gasol was ninth (52.1).

5. Despite being generously listed at 6-foot-9 (he once admitted to TNT he's 6-foot-7), Ben Wallace somehow

finished with 1,729 blocked shots in the 2000s, good for second and only nine behind the 6-foot-11 Duncan.

6. Kevin Garnett recorded a decade-best 71 double-doubles in the 2003-04 season. In six of those games he had at least 20 points and 20 rebounds.

7. Kobe Bryant's 2,173 shot attempts in 2005-06 rank 11th for a single season. Only he and Michael Jordan have taken 2,000 shots in a season over the last 24 years with Jordan taking 2,003 in the 1992-93 season.

8. Ray Allen hit 200 or more 3-pointers five times during the 2000s while playing for three different teams (Seattle, Milwaukee and Boston). He also had 1999 in the 2008-09 season.

9. During the 2005-06 regular season, Dwyane Wade averaged 10.7 free throws per game. In leading the Heat to the NBA title that postseason, he averaged 16.2 in the six-game series against the Mavericks and took 46 in Games 5 and 6.

10. From 2001-06, University of Utah center Andrew Bogut was the only No. 1 overall pick to attend college.

11. Prior to Wade's arrival, the Heat had won three playoff series in their first 15 years in the league. They won seven in his first three seasons.

12. If LeBron James had nine more assists in his 2003-04 rookie

season, he would have averaged at least 6.0 assists in every season of his career.

13. Jason Kapono was the only player to make at least 100 3-pointers and shoot better than 50 percent from beyond the arc in the 2000s, making 108 of 210 in 2006-07 for the Miami Heat.

14. Like the previous two decades, the 2000s was mainly a lost one for the Clippers as they recorded only one winning season. But that 2005-06 campaign was a special one as they won a playoff series for the first time since being located in Buffalo in 1975-76.

15. The 2000-01 Lakers lost only one game en route to the NBA title, an overtime defeat at home in Game 1 of the NBA Finals to the Philadelphia 76ers, and went 8-0 on the road that postseason. Bryant averaged 32.0 points in those games while O'Neal had eight double-doubles and contributed 26.4 points and 13.4 rebounds per game.

TRIVIA TIME

1. How many different players led the league in scoring in the 2000s?

   A. 4
   B. 8
   C. 7
   D. 6

2. How many times did Allen Iverson say the word "practice" during his epic press conference rant during the 2002 playoffs?

   A. 26
   B. 22
   C. 30
   D. 28

3. Shaquille O'Neal was drafted to the NBA in 1992 by which team?

   A. Miami Heat
   B. Orlando Magic
   C. Cleveland Cavaliers
   D. Los Angeles Lakers

4. Allen Iverson had back-to-back 30-point seasons in 2000-01 and 2001-02. Who was the last player before him to accomplish that feat?

    A. Michael Jordan
    B. Shaquille O'Neal
    C. Adrian Dantley
    D. George Gervin

5. Ben Wallace ended his career in 2012 in which team?

    A. Detroit Pistons
    B. Washington Wizards
    C. Chicago Bulls
    D. Orlando Magic

ANSWERS:

1. D
2. B
3. B
4. A
5. A

CHAPTER 6

THE 2010S OR LEBRON'S REIGN OF EXCELLENCE

Final(ly), LeBron

After being denied by "Super Teams" from Boston twice as well as a plucky Orlando Magic team in the 2009 Eastern Conference finals, James knew something had to change in Cleveland or he had to change teams.

While "The Decision" was universally panned as a television spectacle, it also started a run of seven straight NBA Finals appearances for James that continued in 2016-17. To put this in a better perspective, James is only the seventh player in NBA history to accomplish this feat – the other six were from the Celtics dynasties that spanned the late 1950 and early 1960s.

Since "The Return" to Cleveland for the 2014-15 season, James has averaged 29.2 points while the Cavaliers have gone 42-12 and have a chance at a second title in three years. As a franchise, Cleveland has 85 playoff wins in James' 10 seasons. It has 28 without him in the other 38.

Stacking Up 70 Wins

Golden State Warriors coach Steve Kerr is the common thread to the NBA's only 70-win teams in league history. He was a shooting guard on the 1995-96 team that went 72-10, making 51.5 percent of his shots from 3-point range and finishing second to Scottie Pippen in 3-pointers made that season with 122.

He then coached the Warriors to the current standard of 73 wins in the 2015-16 season. That team also had three players to make at least 100 3-pointers, but Stephen Curry and Klay Thompson alone combined for 678 3-pointers, 134 more than the entire Bulls team.

A few things stand out about each standout season. Both teams absorbed a 32-point loss, though five of the Warriors nine defeats came by double-digit margins compared to two for the Bulls. In fact, Chicago's last three losses were all by one point. Chicago dropped back-to-back games once, while Golden State avoided consecutive defeats all season.

But if the ring is the thing, then the Bulls are supreme because they won the title while the Warriors lost to the Cavaliers in seven games.

Trust the Process

It sounds like a meme from the movie "Office Space," but former 76ers general manager Sam Hinkie asked fans to take a leap of faith and believe in his quantitative methods to build the franchise into a contender.

What was the process? Well, it included one of the worst three-year stretches of any team in NBA history as the Sixers won a combined 47 games from 2013-16. In that three-year span, teams put together 34 individual seasons of 48 wins or better

The losing was supposed to result in high lottery picks that would eventually turn the franchise around. Hinkie, however, resigned in April of 2016 after he became marginalized within the organization. But in the end, Hinkie may have been crazy like a fox because the Sixers improved to 28-54 last season and had the No. 3 overall pick in what many consider a loaded 2017 draft.

Gunner Gasol

Throughout his nine-year career, every mention of Marc Gasol's name has been followed by "Pau's younger brother." But the 7-foot-1 Spaniard accomplished a rare feat in 2016-17. He entered the season 12 for 66 (27.3 percent) from 3-point range for his 569-game career, but made 104 of 268 for the season.

He had surpassed his career total by his 10th game of the season as first-year coach David Fizdale saw Gasol with the same potential in range as he did while coaching Chris Bosh with the Heat. Gasol was one of five 7-footers to hit at least 100 3-pointers in 2016-17 and had the best percentage of the bunch at 38.8 percent.

So Nice He Did It Twice

It's rare to see the same career arc play out twice in a basketball player's career, but Jimmy Butler has pulled off the trick. At Marquette, Butler arrived on the Milwaukee campus after transferring twice to follow one-time assistant and eventual head coach Buzz Williams.

In his three years with the Golden Eagles, Butler went from role player off the bench to starter leader as they made the NCAA Tournament all three seasons and reached the regional finals in 2011.

That work ethic impressed the Chicago Bulls enough to make him a late first-round selection in 2011. Again, Butler grinded and hungered to succeed, first in spot minutes as a rookie and then a role player in his second season and a full-time starter in year three.

The last three seasons, though, have seen him blossom into a superstar by averaging at least 20 points and capped by a career-best 23.9 per game in 2016-17. While the Bulls have made the playoffs in all but one of his six seasons, he may be the first highly tradeable superstar because the Bulls seem to be indifferent about the crossroads they're currently at – a team good enough to make the playoffs but not good enough to advance deep in them.

The Black Mamba Snakes Out on a High

Kobe Bryant holds many distinctions in NBA history, but he is unique in the sense he's the only player with a 20-year career with one team. His farewell game against the Utah Jazz to wrap up the 2015-16 season also qualifies as unique considering he scored a season league-high 60 points while putting up a career-high 50 shots.

It was just the fifth time he reached the mark, and he took fewer shots in 2006 when he scored a career-high 81 that ranks as the second-highest total in NBA history. But it was a fitting end to a career in which the 18-time All-Star won five NBA titles, two NBA Finals MVP awards, the 2008 NBA MVP award and a pair of scoring titles.

And because winning mattered most to Bryant, his farewell game also meant the Lakers won all five games he scored 60 or more points.

The $100 Million Men

High-paying contracts are part of any sport, though the NBA seems to have more players than most crossing the $100 million thresholds between the rise of player salaries and the lucrative television deals the league has signed with various media outlets.

A total of 16 players have signed contracts for at least $100 million that included playing years in this decade. Of these 16, however, only Kevin Love has provided the ultimate return of an NBA title, and that was in large part due more to LeBron James than Kevin Love.

Further, Love isn't even the highest-paid player on this list. Between the new TV deal and the Larry Bird exemption that allows a team to re-sign its best player at a higher annual salary than a potential free agent suitor, Grizzlies point guard Mike Conley just completed the first season of his 5-year, $153 million contract.

D'oh, Canada!

If Steve Nash represents everything good about Canadian basketball, then Anthony Bennett is the polar opposite. Bennett became the first Canadian player to be the No. 1 overall selection in the draft when the Cavaliers picked him in 2013. He had played just one year at UNLV, averaging 16.1 points and 8.1 rebounds, and the hope was that Bennett would be like former Runnin' Rebels great Larry Johnson, who had a productive NBA career.

Instead, Bennett wound up being perhaps the worst No. 1 pick in NBA history. He fizzled out after just four starts and 151 games with four different teams. Bennett was traded to Minnesota after his rookie season as part of a three-team deal that sent Kevin Love to Cleveland. The Timberwolves bought out his contract before the start of the 2015-16 season and he signed with his hometown team in Toronto.

Bennett earned the dubious distinction of being the first No. 1 pick to play in the NBA D-League, but he also requested to be sent there. The Raptors cut him before the end of the season. He began 2016-17 with the Brooklyn Nets, who cut him in mid-season.

Bennett then latched on with Turkish club Fenerbahce, and while the club won its first EuroLeague title in club history, they cut the small forward after he totaled 12 points and nine rebounds in 10 games.

The Insanity was Not Drafting Him

Here's a dirty secret about undrafted point guard Jeremy Lin: Everyone knew he was an NBA-caliber point guard despite playing collegiately at Harvard. Lin averaged 15.5 points and 4.1 assists in his final three seasons with the Crimson, who were overshadowed in the Ivy League by Cornell while he played.

He was the first player in Ivy history to finish with 1,450 points, 450 rebounds, 400 assists and 200 steals. Lin was a Bob Cousy Award finalist his senior year. While he didn't get an invite to the NBA Scouting Combine, they took his measurements at the Portsmouth Invitational, and they compared favorably to the league's top point guards in that class.

After watching all 30 teams pass him up twice, he signed as a free agent with Golden State and played 29 games as a rookie. In the 2011-12 season, Lin's life became a whirlwind in December. The Warriors cut him on Dec. 9, and the Rockets signed him three days later. Houston then cut him on Christmas Day, and the Knicks, whose backcourt was decimated by injuries, signed him two days later.

He had more DNPs (11) than games played (9) after being signed before his big break against the Nets on Feb. 4 in which he scored 25 points off the bench. That led to an incredible first five career starts in which he averaged 27.2 points and shot 50.0 percent from the field. By season's end, he averaged 14.6 points—still a career-high – and parlayed that into a 3-year, $25 million offer sheet from the Rockets.

Lin, who has played for six teams in seven seasons, would sign a second big deal, this time with the Hornets for $38 million before the 2015-16 season. The bottom line? Those Harvard guys are always going to find a way to make money.

The Brow and Boogie Show

The biggest trade of the 2016-17 season came when the New Orleans Pelicans, who were hosting the All-Star Game, made a blockbuster deal to acquire DeMarcus Cousins from the Sacramento Kings during that weekend. The deal was finalized the day after Davis was named the MVP of the All-Star game in which he scored 52 points in front of the home fans while

Cousins played sparingly.

The deal put a pair of young, promising power forward-center players together to the way the Spurs used Tim Duncan and David Robinson back in the late 1990s and early 2000s.

The 17-game sample size was a mixed bag. New Orleans went 7-10 in those games as Davis scored 28.3 points per game and Cousins averaged 24.4. Cousins had more rebounds in those games (211-188), and the two combined for 47 blocks.

If there was one immediate positive, it was that Cousins was whistled for just one technical in those 17 games. He had 17 in 55 games with the Kings before the deal was made.

As good as these former Kentucky players are, they may only go as far as the backcourt who can get them the ball in their favorite spots. Because Davis and Cousins have a combined zero playoff wins, with Davis getting swept by the Warriors in the first round in 2015 and Cousins failing to reach the postseason in Sacramento.

RANDOM FACTS AND FIGURES

1. Since the 2010-11 season up to the 2017 NBA Finals, LeBron James has played 141 postseason games. The Minnesota Timberwolves, Phoenix Suns and Sacramento Kings have all failed to reach the playoffs in that span.

2. DeMarcus Cousins has been whistled for 106 technical fouls since entering the league in 2010. By comparison, all San Antonio Spurs players have combined for 63 in that span.

3. Serge Ibaka's four-year run from 2011-14 as the NBA's leader in blocked shots was the longest by any player since Dikembe Mutombo won five straight from 1994-98.

4. Greivis Vazquez's 704 assists to lead the NBA in 2012-13 were the fewest of any 82-game season since Don Buse had 685 for the Indiana Pacers in 1976-77.

5. This season, DeAndre Jordan became the second player in NBA history to lead the league in shooting percentage for five straight seasons, joining Shaquille O'Neal. Jordan has shot 69.0 percent since the start of the 2012-13 season, while O'Neal made 57.7 percent of his shots leading the league from 1998-2002.

6. During their impressive 18-year run of winning at least 50

games every season, including the 66-game lockout-shortened 2011-12 campaign, the Spurs have posted a cumulative 1,040-420 record since the start of the 1999-2000 season for a .712 winning percentage.

7. Fifteen of the 24 wins during Golden State's record-breaking start to the 2015-16 season were by double digits. The Warriors made 15 or more 3-pointers in 10 of those victories.

8. The Golden State Warriors are the only team to eclipse 40 percent from beyond the arc in a season for the decade, hitting at a 41.6 percent clip in 2015-16 and 40.3 percent in 2012-13.

9. The Warriors (2015-16 and 2016-17) and the 2016-17 Rockets are the only teams from this decade since the 1984-85 season to rank in the top 50 for single-season scoring average. And the 115.9 points per game the Warriors scored in the 2016-17 season ranks only 19th on the list in the last 42 years.

10. James Harden and Russell Westbrook are the only players in NBA history to have more than 400 turnovers, with Harden setting a league-mark with 464 in 2016-17 and Westbrook second at 438. The only other player to reach the dubious milestone was George McInnis, who did so in the ABA in 1972-73 and 1974-75.

11. The blocked shot has been a lost art in this decade. Only seven players have topped 200. Sixteen players reached at least 200 in the previous 10 seasons.

12. Russell Westbrook had a single-season NBA record 42 triple-doubles in 2016-17. Not counting James Harden (22) and LeBron James (13), the rest of the NBA had 40.

13. Joel Anthony has played the most games this decade (321) without attempting a 3-pointer.

14. From 2014-2017, Stephen Curry and Klay Thompson have combined to make 1,785 3-pointers, which is more than the Milwaukee Bucks (1,705), Memphis Grizzlies (1,694) and Minnesota Timberwolves (1,462) have in that span.

15. The 2016-17 season marked the first time Kevin Durant had an assist-to-turnover ratio of better than 2-to-1 (2.17).

TRIVIA TIME

1. How many straight seasons has Stephen Curry led the NBA in 3-pointers made?

   A. 3

   B. 4

   C. 5

   D. 6

2. Who is the only player on the current Brooklyn Nets roster to have been with the team since the start of the decade (2010-11)?

   A. Brook Lopez

   B. Randy Foye

   C. Jeremy Lin

   D. Trevor Booker

3. Which one of these players was not a No. 1 overall pick?

   A. Anthony Bennett

   B. Ben Simmons

   C. John Wall

   D. Jabari Parker

4. Who was the last team to make four straight NBA Finals appearances prior to the Miami Heat's run from 2011-14?

A. Boston Celtics

B. Los Angeles Lakers

C. New York Knicks

D. Detroit Pistons

5. Who did Doc Rivers pass to be the all-time winningest coach in Clippers history?

A. Larry Brown

B. Bill Fitch

C. Vinny Del Negro

D. Jack Ramsay

ANSWERS:

1. C

2. A

3. D

4. A

5. C

CHAPTER 7
THE NBA AND THE OLYMPICS

After back-to-back Olympics in which a superpower boycotted the Summer Olympiad (the United States did not field a team in 1980 when the Soviet Union hosted the games in Moscow, and the Russians reciprocated four years later when Los Angeles served as host), the 1988 Olympics in Seoul was to be a defining moment for Team USA in basketball.

In Olympiads past, the U.S. almost always returned home with the gold medal. Their lone Olympic defeat was the hotly disputed 1972 gold medal game against the Soviets in Munich with an ending so controversial the U.S. team not only did not attend the medal ceremony but they also refused to accept their silver medals they were so incensed at what was a chaotic final three seconds that allowed the Soviets, in their eyes, to steal the gold.

But the U.S. basketball machine resumed rolling in 1976 and 1984, winning gold medals to restore order. The 1988 team was another collection of standout college All-Stars that was led by Kansas forward Danny Manning, who willed the Jayhawks to the

NCAA Tournament title that spring with such a dominant effort the team was called "Danny and the Miracles."

Other future NBA stars on the team included David Robinson, Mitch Richmond, Hersey Hawkins, Stacey Augmon and Dan Majerle, with Georgetown coach John Thompson bringing along his point guard Charles Smith as part of the 12-man roster.

In the semifinals, the U.S. and the Soviet Union met in the semifinals, and this time, the upset was a legitimate victory for the Russians. Led by 7-foot-3 center Arvydas Sabonis, who would eventually play for the Portland Trail Blazers later in his career, an older, crisp-passing Soviet squad had little trouble breaking the full-court press of the young, athletic U.S. team and led almost wire-to-wire in an 82-76 victory.

The U.S. regrouped to thump Australia to win the bronze medal, but it was still the worst performance in Olympic history. It also wound up making a greater global appeal for professionals to play in the Olympics, something both the U.S. and the Soviets ironically voted against when the rules changed in 1989 ahead of the 1992 Barcelona games.

Barcelona (1992) – The Original "Dream Team"

Despite the rule change, the NBA was initially lukewarm to the idea of its players participating in the Olympics. The "Dream Team" nickname originally came about eight months before the first 10 players of the team were actually selected – Sports Illustrated coined the phrase as part of its cover for the February 18, 1991, issue that looked at what a potential roster could be.

By the time September rolled around, USA Basketball had its first 10 players. There were two sets of teammates: Michael Jordan and Scottie Pippen from the Chicago Bulls, and Karl Malone and John Stockton from the Utah Jazz. Despite dealing with back ailments and being 35 years old, Larry Bird was selected because he was still one of the NBA's best players. Robinson returned for his second Olympics and arguably was the most motivated given what had happened in Seoul, while Jordan, Patrick Ewing and Chris Mullin all were trying to win a second gold medal after doing so in Los Angeles in 1984.

Magic Johnson and Charles Barkley rounded out the initial 10, and Johnson remained on the team despite retiring from the NBA two months after his announcement he tested positive for HIV. Barkley, like Malone, were both cut during tryouts for the 1984 team by Indiana coach Bobby Knight and also entered the team with chips on their shoulder.

Because one of the remaining two spots would go to a college player, the two remaining pros vying for the 11th spot on the roster were Clyde Drexler and Isiah Thomas. By this point, It was a well-known fact in the NBA that Jordan had a long memory, and the "freeze-out" Thomas conducted in the 1985 All-Star game came into play here. Both Jordan and Pippen lobbied hard against Thomas, and they eventually got their Olympic teammates to fall in line.

Another strike against Thomas was how the Pistons refused to congratulate the Bulls after Jordan's team swept them in the 1991 Eastern Conference finals. That didn't sit well with the NBA hierarchy, but in Jackie MacMullan's book "When the Game was Ours," Johnson described the view from his peers that made the decision easier.

"Nobody on that team wanted to play with him," Johnson said of Thomas. "Michael didn't want to play with him. Scottie wanted no part of him. Bird wasn't pushing for him. Karl Malone didn't want him. Who was saying, 'We need this guy?' Nobody."

So Drexler was on the team. The last spot came down to LSU center Shaquille O'Neal and Duke forward Christian Laettner. While O'Neal would eventually go first in the 1992 draft and Laettner would be No. 3, it was Laettner's championship pedigree that earned him the nod from USA Basketball. He won a pair of NCAA Tournament titles in 1991 and 1992 with the Blue Devils and had made the Final Four the previous two seasons.

The practices led by Pistons and USA coach Chuck Daly were legendary, but the cohesion of such an incredible group of talent didn't come right away. Daly, in fact, pulled an outstanding coaching maneuver in June of 1992 to prove his team wasn't invincible.

It was admittedly difficult to come up with opposition that could give this collection of talent a challenge. USA Basketball came up with a college All-Star team, one that arguably would have been comprised the Olympic squad had the rules to allow professionals been shot down. Two of Laettner's Duke teammates, Bobby Hurley and Grant Hill were on the team, along with future NBA stars Penny Hardaway (Memphis State), Allan Houston (Tennessee), Chris Webber (Michigan) and Eric Montross (North Carolina).

The wide-eyed college kids took in practice before facing the pros in a scrimmage in California, yet somehow they pulled off an upset victory. Duke coach Mike Krzyzewski, an assistant on the team, later admitted Daly intentionally limited Jordan's minutes and had an irregular substitution pattern to drive home a point. The next day, the teams played again, and the Dream Team ran the college kids off the court.

The other key competition was an intrasquad scrimmage in Monaco that Jordan called "the best game I was ever in." Daly purposely put Jordan and Johnson on separate teams and let them go full-bore at each other in a 20-minute scrimmage in an empty gym. Jordan's team won 40-36 in what has been labeled "the Greatest Game Nobody Ever Saw."

One of the upshots of the Dream Team was the arrival of Barkley as a star. Never at a loss for words, Barkley became a folk hero of sorts because he wandered around Barcelona without security. Jordan did as Jordan does, ruthlessly playing cards against teammates and multiple rounds of golf as time permitted.

As for the games themselves? The U.S. won their eight games by an average of 43.8 points. They opened with a 116-48 out of Angola, a game made infamous by Barkley's intentional elbow of Herlander Coimbra that resulted in the "1" of a 46-1 run by the U.S. Jordan and Pippen settled a personal vendetta against future teammate and Croatian Toni Kukoc, whom Bulls general manager Jerry Krause had drafted and was part of a bargaining chip used against Pippen in contract negotiations.

The Dream Team was so dominant that Daly did not have to call a timeout in the eight games. Only Croatia and Puerto Rico lost by less than 40 points. Barkley shot 71.1 percent and averaged a team-high 18 points. All was right with the U.S. basketball world again.

Atlanta (1996) – Dream Team III

In some ways, the 1996 U.S. Olympic squad, dubbed "Dream Team III" (Dream Team II was the 1994 squad that competed in the FIBA World Championships in Toronto) was in a no-win situation. Like the 1992 team, they would be overwhelming favorites to win the gold medal, but they were also trying to live up to an impossible standard set four years prior in Barcelona. And they were the host team with the Olympics in Atlanta.

Five of the players were holdovers from the 1992 team: Barkley, Malone, Pippen, Robinson and Stockton. Coach Lenny Wilkens opted for size with his roster, enlisting fellow 7-footers O'Neal and Hakeem Olajuwon to join Robinson. His team also had plenty of ball-handling flexibility with height in Pippen, Hill, Hardaway and Reggie Miller.

You can make the argument that Gary Payton was the worst player on this team, and he was not only considered the second-best point guard of the 1990s, but he was far and away the most tenacious defensive point guard of his era. Nicknamed "The Glove," Payton took a borderline sadistic glee in playing defense, and backed up his elite skill set with equally elite trash-talking.

Wilkens was far more laid-back than Daly, and the result was a team that, while supremely talented, was a bunch of individuals far more than the team that bonded together in 1992. Barkley was quick to notice the difference between the squads and called the process of getting his second gold medal "a nightmare."

"It was not a lot of fun hearing guys (moan) and complain all the time about who should be starting," he said in a podcast for SiriusXM Bleacher Report Radio in 2016. "In '96, guys started complaining about playing time — guys started (saying), 'well I should be starting.' And I'm like 'wait a minute, Y'all (aren't) even that good compared to the team I used to be on."

Whatever chemistry it lacked, it sure didn't show in the results.

The U.S. won all eight of its games by at least 23 points, with Pippen again tormenting Kukoc in group play as part of a 102-71 win. Barkley again led the U.S. in scoring, averaging 12.4 points as nine players scored at least 9.4 points per game in the eight lopsided victories.

Sydney (2000) – The Transition Team and "The Dunk of Death"

At the turn of the millennium, the U.S. was now 101-2 in Olympic basketball and two-time defending champions. The job of restoring the Americans to their rightful stop atop the global pecking order officially done, it was time to find a new generation of stars to carry the (pardon the pun) Olympic torch.

Coach Rudy Tomjanovich had only one holdover from the 1996 squad with Payton. But this team was lacking the pizazz and oomph of the previous two squads. The qualifying process in 1999 showed that Jason Kidd and Kevin Garnett were ready to be part of the core, but other players such as Houston, Tim Hardaway, Vin Baker and Tom Gugliotta didn't really move the needle with the public.

In retrospect, the omissions from the 2000 squad on paper look like they could have manhandled the team that went to Australia. O'Neal, Robinson, Pippen, Malone, Stockton, Miller, Kobe Bryant, Tim Duncan and Allen Iverson were all bypassed, though to be fair, veterans such as Malone and O'Neal weren't overly interested in making another Olympic appearance.

The last spot originally went to Ray Allen, which left both Iverson and Vince Carter raw. When the announcement was made, Iverson promptly scored 46 points against Allen and the Milwaukee Bucks just to prove a point. Carter also took his frustrations out on Allen and the Bucks, scoring 47 as his Raptors teammates made it a point to hammer Allen all game long and left him with a black eye and bloody nose.

Carter, was already in the marketing machines of becoming a star thanks to his impressive array of vicious dunks that made him appear to be the logical evolution to Jordan's high-flying days. But he made his way onto the team only after Gugliotta suffered a knee injury that would force him to miss the Olympics.

Where the previous Olympic teams carried a swagger that opposing countries feared, the Sydney Games marked the first real tournament in which the world was catching up to USA Basketball. As center Alonzo Mourning noted, "That was like the first year where we noticed the competition just didn't fear us anymore."

Additionally, Mourning was going through his own physical issues at the time and it would eventually turn out he would need a kidney transplant.

This U.S. team may have been the tightest of the first three squads because to a man, they all rallied to protect the precocious Carter, who was having a brutal year off the court with family and legal issues he was not directly involved in. Carter's athleticism was unlike anything anyone had seen, and even his peers were slack-jawed at what he could do against them in practice.

That translated into the games, where Carter tried to dunk on everyone. Opposing players noted this and responded by trying to undercut him as he slashed into the lane, further fostering the "us against the world" mentality this team had.

In group play, the U.S. had its first legitimate contest in the era of NBA players as it fought off Lithuania 85-76 in the third game. Carter scored six points in the final 2:45, but Lithuania lost this game more than the U.S. won it. They missed 16 free throws, including a pair by Eurelijus Zukauskas with 69 seconds left that could have made it a 3-point game and held the U.S. to 35.7 percent shooting.

The U.S. regrouped to pound New Zealand, but it was the final group play game against France that would be remembered for what the French call "le dunk de la morte," a posterizing dunk witnessed millions of times on YouTube since there were only still photos when news shows provided Olympic updates due to rights contracts.

The U.S. held a comfortable 15-point lead early in the second half when Carter jumped a passing lane in the frontcourt to intercept an outlet pass. He attacked the rim from an angle on the left side, and in his path was France's 7-foot-2 center Frederic Weis, a first-round pick of the New York Knicks.

Weis froze, and Carter needed just two dribbles to pick up a full head of steam at him and the basket. Weis never left his feet as Carter took off, and as he recounted in a 2015 interview with ESPN, "If I get up in the air before you jump, you don't have a shot in hell to stop me."

In addition to his staggering vertical leap, Carter further propelled himself higher by pushing off on Weis' shoulder. As he continued towards the basket, Weis ducked his head slightly, but it was still Carter essentially playing leapfrog with a standing 7-foot-2 inch human being before throwing down a one-handed dunk that stunned everyone in the arena in Sydney – fans, media, opponents, Carter's teammates and even Carter himself.

Garnett had possibly the funniest reaction to the dunk, first watching with his mouth open as Carter soared over Weis and then grabbing Carter's head and rolling it as the two celebrated screaming. Carter was so excited he almost punched Garnett right after he came down while he swung wildly in celebration.

The U.S. eventually won that game and another gold medal, but the road was difficult. Lithuania, coached by Donn Nelson, the son of then-Dallas Mavericks coach Don Nelson, gave them an even tougher ride in the semifinals and had a potential game-winning 3-pointer fall short in an 85-83 defeat. Carter put the

U.S. ahead for good with a tough baseline jumper with 31 seconds left, and Antonio McDyess had a putback of a missed free throw by Garnett to make it 84-81. Sarunas Jasikevicius, who played collegiately at Maryland, drew Lithuania within one, and after a free throw by Kidd, Jasikevicius went for glory and a 22-footer that fell just wide of the mark.

The U.S. and France would meet again, this time for the gold medal, and while Weis did the right thing and fouled Carter on his way up for a dunk, the U.S. emerged with an 85-75 win and a third straight gold.

Athens (2004) – The World Catches Up

By the time the Athens Games rolled around, it was clear the NBA was an international game, and foreign players toiling in the NBA were making their national teams better. Spain and Argentina were at the forefront of the global revolution, their veteran pass-oriented squads a perfect foil for the assembled collection of individual talent the U.S. would put together in a bid to win gold.

Larry Brown, who was an assistant to Tomjanovich in Sydney, took the reins as head coach and assembled a very young team – Iverson was the oldest player at 29, and six of the players were 22 or younger, including a 19-year-old named LeBron James who had just finished a solid rookie season and averaged 20.9 points. But again, a deeper look at the players who weren't making the trip for various reasons – Carter, Kidd, Allen, Bryant, Elton Brand – forced Brown's hand somewhat.

Additionally, everyone knew the U.S. was ripe for the picking. The team finished sixth in the FIBA World Championships in 2002 and there were only three holdovers from the team that qualified the U.S. for the Olympics in the tournament of the Americas earlier in 2004. And now here was Brown with a team he couldn't relate to – one comprised of youngsters versus his preference of veterans.

Brown, who nearly sent Stephon Marbury home in a fit of rage after he found out what Marbury had said to a reporter about his coaching style, felt like he had to coach this team in every facet of the game, down to the fundamentals, and the players resisted. It had all the makings of a disaster, and sure enough, it all came to fruition.

It started right off the bad as the U.S. was embarrassed by Puerto Rico 92-73 in the first game. A Puerto Rico team that had two NBA players held the U.S. to 3 of 24 shooting from 3-point range and 35 percent shooting overall. Somehow, the U.S. forgot Duncan was the most formidable frontcourt player in the world and got him only 10 shots. They trailed by 22 at halftime, and aside from a brief spurt to close within eight, looked helplessly out of sorts in their worst loss in Olympic history.

Every game in group play save the finale against Angola was a struggle. The U.S. battled past host Greece 77-71 in front of an obviously partisan and hostile crowd. In an oral history for a GQ article, James said "that was the loudest arena I've ever been in." The U.S. was 2-2 in group play after a 94-90 setback to Lithuania, in which Jasikevicius got a measure of revenge for the semifinal loss in Sydney.

The U.S. didn't play like a team until the medal round, and its lackluster group play put them opposite Spain in the quarterfinals. The Spaniards rolled through their group with five wins in as many games and were led by Pau Gasol. Marbury, embattled at this point after making just 6 of 30 shots in group play, hit six 3-pointers and set a U.S. Olympic record with 31 points in a hard-fought 102-94 win.

The Americans had finally found some success against zone defenses after misfiring throughout group play, sinking 12 of 22 from beyond the arc. Defensively, the U.S. held Gasol to four fourth-quarter points after he scored 25 in the first three.

The semifinal against Argentina, though, was the same old story for the U.S. An inability to hit from the outside, Duncan in early foul trouble and no one else stepped up offensively in an 89-81 upset by the South American country. San Antonio Spurs guard Manu Ginobili had 29 points and former Temple guard Pepe Sanchez controlled the tempo of the game as the Argentines showed their 2002 victory over a U.S. team comprised of NBA players at the FIBA Worlds was no fluke.

Brown was criticized for giving limited playing time to James,

Wade and Anthony as well as constricting Kidd at the point. The level of dysfunction on this team was so great that NBA commissioner David Stern agreed with Marbury that the U.S. should have been playing a more up-tempo style.

The U.S. would settle for bronze in its worst Olympic tournament, period, full stop. Two losses became five, and now USA Basketball director Jerry Colangelo had to rebuild the program virtually from scratch. Thus, the seeds were planted for "The Redeem Team."

Beijing (2008) – Rebuilding and "The Redeem Team"

The biggest takeaway from the Athens debacle was that USA Basketball could no longer just put together a team in the summer, roll out a basketball onto the court and expect it to bring home the gold medal. It became painfully clear that the U.S. would now have to use the entire four-year cycle to not only build a team, but to build a player pool from which to create that team.

The man who had to come up with the plan was Jerry Colangelo, hired as the managing director of the senior men's program in 2005. His first act was arguably his most important one, hiring Krzyzewski as head coach. Here was an original link to the 1992 "Dream Team," since the all-time winningest coach in Division I men's basketball was an assistant to Daly and watched him juggle the egos of 11 of the greatest players in NBA history.

Colangelo's other important move within USA Basketball was making himself as the sole decision-maker when it comes to picking the player pool and picking the coaching staff. In previous Olympics, there was a selection committee that voted on the final 12. That was gone.

The last step was the most challenging one, getting players on board to make a three-year commitment. Colangelo went on a tour of the NBA landscape with the following message: If you want to play for the U.S. team, you have to commit for the entire three-year international cycle. No FIBA, no Olympics. No Tournament of the Americas, no Olympics. It was his way or the highway.

But as a long-time player in the NBA as the general manager, president and owner of the Phoenix Suns, Colangelo had a sterling reputation within the league and was well-respected by the players. It made the sell to players such as Bryant, James, Wade and Kevin Durant easy despite the heavy minutes they would log chasing NBA titles before sacrificing their summers for international glory.

There were some growing pains at first as the U.S. finished third in the 2006 FIBA World Championships. But as it turned out, that semifinal defeat would be the only loss during Colangelo's tenure in charge as USA Basketball rebuilt itself into the powerhouse it originally started as when pros were first allowed to participate in the Olympics.

So with the machinations behind the scenes and on the sidelines in place, it was now on the players to figure out how to play together. And the key to it all, ironically enough, was Bryant.

He had missed the 2004 Olympics because of his sexual assault trial in Colorado, but had longed to be a part of the U.S. national team. Colangelo, though, was wary considering Bryant's dominant ball-handling with the Lakers would be a detriment to a team with so much talent. But after a brief conversation in 2006 when Bryant expressed he would accept whatever role asked of him, Colangelo was satisfied the Lakers superstar would work out just fine.

What no one expected, though, was the kind of work ethic Bryant brought to the team in the summer of 2008. While people know Bryant is an offensive juggernaut to sometimes the point of excess, he also has a work ethic that rivals Jordan's on-court ruthlessness in practices. Bryant has always a been an in-first, out-last player when it comes to practice, and to see him doing so shortly after losing to the Celtics in the 2008 NBA Finals set the tone for the rest of the team.

"We all clung to it," Carlos Boozer told the Orange County Register. "It soon became our workout, not just his workout."

Bryant was eager to learn from his fellow stars. He credited Kidd with helping him learn to catch and shoot, a talent that was somewhat lost on Bryant as his career evolved because he was so used to creating his shot off the dribble with the Lakers. His inner drive, combined with his reserved personality, proved to be the perfect personality mesh with his 2008 teammates. Bryant embraced the role of being the defensive stopper on the U.S., and he was the on-court face of this team. That was evident in the team's group play game against Spain in which Bryant plowed his Lakers teammate Gasol to the floor when the 7-footer tried to set a screen.

That was the defining moment for the team as it barreled forward, finishing group play with a rout of Germany followed by lopsided medal-round wins over Australia and Argentina. And all that hard work paid off in the gold medal rematch against Spain. The final score shows a 118-107 win, but the game itself was a much tighter contest of high-quality basketball.

Wade scored a team-high 27 points, but Bryant delivered several clutch plays in the fourth quarter, including a four-point play that both blunted a charge by Spain but also fouled out Rudy Fernandez in the process. When Bryant hit a runner with 1:23 to play, it effectively closed out the Spaniards and got the U.S. back to the top of the basketball world.

London (2012) – Gold Medal Calling

With a foundation now in place, the challenge for the U.S. was to stay atop the basketball world. Krzyzewski opted to return for a second tour of duty as head coach, and many players were willing to come back. But injuries reduced the number of holdovers to five: James, Anthony, Bryant, Chris Paul and Deron Williams.

Wade, Bosh and Dwight Howard were all recovering from injuries, and Blake Griffin made a late exit after suffering a knee injury practicing with the national team. James Harden and Anthony Davis were late additions to round out the roster, as likely participants Derrick Rose and LaMarcus Aldridge were both sidelined by injuries.

Losing Howard, Griffin and Aldridge left the U.S. team thin at the center position. While they did have 7-foot-1 Tyson Chandler, his offensive game was severely limited. Durant and Kevin Love were both 6-foot-10 forwards and interior defense was not their forte, and while Davis had plenty of potential as the No. 1 overall pick in 2012, he was still just 19 years old.

Colangelo thought, however, that what this team lacked in size it more than compensated for with speed and perimeter shooting. It also had some chemistry with Durant, Harden and Russell Westbrook all teammates with the Oklahoma City Thunder and all were 23 or younger.

James took the leadership mantle from Bryant, but the Lakers star still had plenty left to give in what turned out to be his last Olympic go-round. Both Bryant and Krzyzewski announced these would be their last Olympics, though Krzyzewski would later have a change of heart and coach the team in Rio four years later.

The U.S. started slowly in its first two group play games but still blew out France and Tunisia. Krzyzewski went old-school on the team against the Tunisians, benching his starters to start the second half, and the second unit led by Love, Anthony and Westbrook broke open a 13-point game at halftime with a 21-3 run.

The game against Nigeria was a throwback to the 1992 glory days as the U.S. demolished the Super Eagles 156-73. The game will forever be remembered for Anthony blistering Nigeria with 10 3-pointers in 12 attempts and scoring 37 points in just 14 minutes. The U.S. set Olympic records for first-half points (78), total points (156), 3-pointers made (29), field goals (59), shooting percentage (71) and margin of victory (83).

The next game was a complete opposite as the U.S. fought off Lithuania 99-94. The U.S. trailed with less than six minutes to play, but James took over as a scorer, netting nine of his 20 points in the final four minutes. Lithuania exposed the U.S defense's inability to guard the high pick-and-roll, but superior American depth allowed them to make plays down the stretch and avoid the upset.

The march to the gold medal resumed with three more lopsided victories, including a pair over Argentina by a combined 55 points. James had the first triple-double in U.S. Olympic history in the quarterfinal rout of Australia, and Bryant showed he still had game by drilling six 3-pointers in the second half.

The gold medal game was a rematch of the 2008 final against Spain, and it was another close affair won by the U.S. 107-100. James had a key dunk and 3-pointer late to seal the victory, and Durant became the first U.S. player to score 30 points in a gold medal game. James also did yeoman work on the defensive end, often guarding either Pau or Marc Gasol due to the lack of size in the American frontcourt.

For James, it also capped a banner year in which he joined Jordan as the only players to win the NBA MVP award, an NBA title, the NBA Finals MVP and the Olympic gold medal.

Rio de Janeiro (2016) – A Basketball Carnevale

After announcing in London it would be his last Olympics, Krzyzewski insisted as late as February the following year he would not return as U.S. coach. Colangelo asked Krzyzewski to hold off on making a final decision until after Duke completed its 2012-13 season. He had nothing left to prove with a 75-1 mark since taking stewardship of the program, but the more he thought about remaining committed to coaching the Blue Devils, the more he felt he should remain coach of the national team as well.

"I'm 66. I wasn't sure how long I was going to coach," Krzyzewski said in an interview with Sports Illustrated in 2013. "(Now) I'm sure I'm going to coach a while, through the Olympics. You shouldn't be a retired coach coaching the national team. You should be an active coach. It's too cutting edge. You have to be on the firing line."

In this cycle, there would be heavy turnover to the U.S. team as only Anthony and Durant returned. Though he considered returning for a run at a third gold medal with Krzyzewski, Bryant backed away late after his farewell from the NBA included a 60-point, 50-shot performance in his last game. Davis, Griffin, Aldridge and Stephen Curry all were out due to injuries, while James, Paul, Harden and Westbrook withdrew themselves from consideration.

Additionally, Howard, Love and Andre Iguodala were among the final cuts when the roster was cut to the final 12. Much like the 2012 team, the U.S. did not have an overwhelming collection of height – only DeAndre Jordan and DeMarcus Cousins were taller than 6-foot-9, but there was plenty of perimeter firepower that included a reunion of Krzyzewski with his one-time Duke point guard Kyrie Irving.

Though Curry was unavailable, the Warriors were well represented on the heels of their 73-win season with Klay Thompson and Draymond Green, and the Toronto Raptors starting backcourt of Kyle Lowry and DeMar DeRozan were also part of the U.S. roster. Anthony was now the U.S. elder statesman at 32, and the Olympics were his personal happy place.

The biggest reason why Anthony loves playing in the Olympics is that he has always been the finisher for the U.S. He doesn't have to worry about the flow of the offense, he creates mismatches for the opposing team's forwards – his low-post footwork is exquisite – or centers – he can drag your big man out to the perimeter and shoot over him anytime he likes -- and works within the framework teammates create for him.

"I can just kind of space out, take my time, pick my spots and play off the guys that I have on my team," he told NBA.com. "That's all it's been. It's just a matter of picking your spots and playing off your teammates."

The first two games were heavy mismatches as the U.S. beat China and Venezuela by a combined 101 points while averaging 116.0. Anthony scored 31 points as the U.S. fought off a tough Australian team and then a dogged and veteran Serbian squad gave it fits before a potential game-tying 3-pointer missed and allowed the U.S. to escape with a 94-91 win.

The 50th straight international win in all competitions was no cakewalk either as the U.S. held off France 100-97 thanks to 30 points from Thompson. What the U.S. lacked in terms of a consistent go-to scorer was canceled out by the fact that five different players led the team in scoring in the five group play games.

The quarterfinals brought a much-needed blowout as the U.S. rolled through Argentina 105-78, with Durant scoring 27 as the

Americans saw the last of the Ginobili-led "Golden Generation" of Argentines who will forever be remembered for their 2004 gold medal in Athens that forced the U.S. rethink.

Spain loomed once more in the semifinals, and much like the Argentines before them, the best of La Furia Roja put up a determined challenge before falling 82-76. It was a gritty game, but Thompson scored just enough points (22) and Jordan grabbed just enough rebounds (16) to keep Pau Gasol and Spain at bay.

The gold medal game was a rematch against Serbia, and this time there would be no close calls. Durant hit a 3-pointer to end the first quarter, and the U.S. unleashed 10 minutes of fury on the Serbs in the second, outscoring them 33-14 to take a 52-29 halftime lead. Durant scored 30, duplicating his feat from London, Krzyzewski rode off into the international sunset with his third gold as head coach and fourth overall and a perfect 24-0 record in the Olympics. All's well that ends well.

RANDOM FACTS AND FIGURES

1. Anthony is currently the all-time U.S. leader in points (336), rebounds (125) and field goals made (113). He's also the only four-time medalist for the U.S. men's team, winning three golds to go with his bronze in 2004.

2. DeAndre Jordan was one of the unsung players in Rio, averaging 7.4 points and a team-high 6.1 rebounds while shooting 74.2 percent (23 of 31) from the field.

3. Of Carter's 41 baskets in the 2008 games, 25 were dunks. He also was tied for second on the team with 11 3-pointers.

4. The 1992 "Dream Team" shot 57.8 percent from the field while averaging 117.3 points.

5. In a case of Michael Jordan being Michael Jordan, he said his biggest takeaway from being on the 1992 team was learning the weaknesses of Barkley, Malone and Stockton. He beat each of them in the NBA Finals during Chicago's second "three-peat."

6. Barkley shot an unfathomable 74.4 percent (90 for 121) in his two Olympic appearances. A career 26.6 percent 3-point shooter in the NBA, he was 9 of 12 from long range in Barcelona and Atlanta.

7. The 2004 and 2016 squads were the only ones of the seven

not to shoot at least 50 percent, but the 2004 team was the gang that couldn't shoot straight as its 45.9 percent overall and 31.4 percent from 3-point range are the worst of any U.S. teams since the pros began playing.

8. Lost in the offensive devastation of the 1992 team was that it played some strong defense. Everyone but Stockton recorded at least seven steals and the U.S. held opponents to 36.5 percent shooting in those eight wins.

9. Anthony's status as the all-time leading scorer for the U.S. is tenuous at best. If Durant decides to suit up for a try at a third gold medal, he needs just 26 points to pass 'Melo.

10. Durant has two more 3-pointers (59) than Anthony despite attempting 31 fewer shots (108) from beyond the arc.

11. James is tied for fifth on the all-time blocked shots list for the U.S. despite having only 10.

12. Since losing to Argentina in the 2004 semifinals, the U.S. has won the last four Olympic games between the teams by an average of 25.5 points.

13. Anthony is the only Syracuse alum to play for the U.S. senior men's basketball team.

14. Allan Houston shot better from 3-point range (12 of 20) than he did from 2-point range (6 of 18) in 2000.

15. The 2012 U.S. team ranked first in every offensive category except free throw percentage.

TRIVIA TIME

1. Besides Mike Krzyzewski, who were the other two assistants to Chuck Daly on the 1992 U.S. staff?
   A. P.J. Carlesimo and Jim Boeheim
   B. Phil Jackson and Pat Riley
   C. Larry Brown and George Karl
   D. P.J. Carlesimo and Lenny Wilkens

2. How many players on the 2008 U.S. team did NOT play collegiately?
   A. 1
   B. 2
   C. 3
   D. 4

3. In which NCAA Final Four did 1992 Dream Team teammates Chris Mullin and Patrick Ewing square off?
   A. 1984
   B. 1985
   C. 1986
   D. 1987

4. Australian Joe Ingles launched his NBA career in 2014, playing for which team?
   A. Utah Jazz
   B. Cleveland Cavaliers

C. Golden State Warriors

D. San Antonio Spurs

5. Which country was the first to lose to the U.S. team by single digits after the rules change that allowed professional players to participate?

A. Lithuania

B. Greece

C. Argentina

D. Spain

ANSWERS:

1. D
2. C
3. B
4. A
5. A

DON'T FORGET YOUR
FREE BOOKS

GET THEM FOR FREE ON WWW.TRIVIABILL.COM

MORE BOOKS BY BILL O'NEILL

I hope you enjoyed this book and learned something new.

Please feel free to check out some of my previous books.

Made in the USA
San Bernardino, CA
14 December 2019